Who is Jesus the Christ?

BY

Peter Husbands

Who is Jesus the Christ?

Copyright © 2025 by Peter Husbands
Cover design and edits by Candace Paul

All rights reserved. No part of this publication may be reproduced, distributed, or transmitted in any form or by any means, including photocopying, recording, or other electronic or mechanical methods, without the prior written permission of the author, except in the case of brief quotations embodied in critical reviews and certain other noncommercial uses permitted by copyright law. For permission requests, write to the publisher addressed "Attention: Publisher" at the email address below.

ISBN: 978-1-7377860-3-0

Ordering Information:
Quantity sales. Special discounts are available on quantity purchases by churches, associations, and others. For details, contact the author at the address below.
Orders by U.S. trade bookstores and wholesalers. Please email admin@aknowingspirit.com.

Dedication

To my family and those seeking truth.

TABLE OF CONTENTS

Dedication

i

Preface

ii

Introduction

iii

CHAPTER ONE

JESUS THE WORD

1

CHAPTER TWO

JESUS THE ROCK

19

CHAPTER THREE

JESUS THE SACRIFICE

67

CHAPTER FOUR

JESUS THE RISEN LORD

87

CHAPTER FIVE
JESUS THE SAVIOUR
105
CHAPTER SIX
JESUS THE SON OF GOD
125
CHAPTER SEVEN
JESUS THE REDEEMER
145
CHAPTER EIGHT
RELATIONSHIP WITH JESUS
157

Preface

This beautifully captures the essence of a true journey of faith—a longing not only to know about Jesus intellectually, but to truly understand who He is and cultivate a personal relationship with Him. The focus on Jesus as more than a figure in history, but as the living Savior and the cornerstone of faith, sets a powerful tone for the message of this book.

My emphasis on seeking the truth through Scripture is particularly compelling. In a world where many voices offer conflicting interpretations of Jesus, returning to the Word of God is essential for understanding His identity and purpose. As Jesus Himself said, "I am the way, the truth, and the life. No one comes to the Father except through Me" (John 14:6). This verse underscores that knowing Him personally is the foundation of our faith and the key to eternal life.

This dedication also acknowledges that what truly matters is not what others say about Jesus, but who He is to each individual. This personal encounter and recognition of Jesus as the Christ is transformative. It invites readers not only to learn but also to reflect, believe, and act—to walk in the way Jesus has shown us.

Our closing words inspire action, encouraging readers to rededicate their lives to His work. This invitation resonates deeply with the call to discipleship and aligns with Jesus' own invitation: "Come, follow me" (Matthew 4:19). It reminds us that knowing Jesus is not a passive experience but an active, life-changing commitment to live for Him and His kingdom.

May this book guide many to a deeper understanding of Jesus, fostering renewed faith and a vibrant relationship with Him.

CHAPTER ONE
JESUS THE WORD THE WORD

The question of who Jesus is has become a central topic of discussion, reflection, and debate. Many perspectives attempt to explain His nature—whether He is God, merely a prophet, or something else, entirely unique and indescribable. Despite debates and various perspectives, the Bible offers specific insights into Jesus' identity that clarifies the Christian understanding of Him as both fully God and fully man, and part of the mystery Christians call the Trinity, or the "three in one."

Jesus as fully God and fully Man

According to Scripture, Jesus as "fully God and fully Man" is God incarnate—God in human form. John 1:1-3 says, "In the beginning was the Word, and the Word was with God, and the Word was God."

Later, in John 1:14, it says, "The Word became flesh and made his dwelling among us." This passage confirms that Jesus is not only with God but is God Himself, taking on human nature to live among us. Philippians 2:6-7 also explains that, while Jesus was equal with God, He chose to humble Himself by becoming human.

Jesus' Role in the Trinity

The concept of the "three in one" refers to the Christian doctrine of the Trinity—Father, Son (Jesus), and Holy Spirit. While the Bible does not use the word "Trinity," it shows the Father, Son, and Holy Spirit working as one unified essence—each having distinct roles, yet remaining one God. Matthew 28:19 describes this unity when Jesus commands His disciples to baptize "in the name of the Father and of the Son and of the Holy Spirit." This demonstrates the equality and oneness shared by all three.

Jesus' Divinity and His Unique Role

Jesus Himself made claims that point to His divine nature. In John 10:30, He declares, "I and the Father are one." This statement affirms His equality with God, and His listeners understood it as such. Jesus was also referred to as "the Son of God" (Matthew 16:16), and in John 8:58, He uses the divine name, "I AM"—the same name God used to identify Himself to Moses.

Jesus as More Than a Prophet

Although Jesus was a great teacher and prophet, the Bible presents Him as much more. Prophets pointed people to God, but Jesus not only pointed to God—He claimed to be God, able to forgive sins (Mark 2:5-7), perform miracles, and offer eternal life (John 14:6). His resurrection is the ultimate proof of His divine authority and power, demonstrating that He has victory over death itself.

Final Thoughts on Jesus

According to the Bible, Jesus is not merely a prophet or just a man, but is the Son of God—fully divine and fully human, and part of the holy Trinity. The "three in one" represents the mystery of one God in three persons, each distinct yet unified. This shows us a complete and relational understanding of God. The Bible invites believers to approach this mystery of faith by trusting in Jesus as the one who bridges humanity and God, offers salvation through His life, death, and resurrection.

In the beginning was the Word, and the Word was with God, and the Word was God. The same was in the beginning with God.
John 1: 1-2 KJV

Understanding who Jesus is requires examining the entirety of Scripture. Every verse, chapter, and book, contributes to a comprehensive picture of Jesus as the Messiah, the Son of God, and the Savior of the world. The Bible reveals truths about Jesus in many interconnected ways, showing that His identity is a profound mystery that spans from eternity to His time on earth.

In the Gospel of John, we see this clearly in the opening verses: "In the beginning was the Word, and the

Word was with God, and the Word was God" (John 1:1). John's use of the term "Word" (or Logos in Greek) speaks to Jesus' eternal existence. The Logos was with God, indicating distinct personhood, yet the Logos was also fully God. This highlights that Jesus, while one with God, is also unique in His role within the Godhead. John 1:3 confirms this by stating, "Through him all things were made; without him nothing was made that has been made." Jesus is presented as the divine agent of creation—the one through whom everything came into existence.

The prophet Micah also speaks of the eternality of Jesus. In Micah 5:2, it is prophesied that the Messiah would come from Bethlehem, but is one "whose origins are from of old, from ancient times." This points to His pre-existence—long before His birth in Bethlehem. Jesus existed as the eternal Word with God.

By studying the whole of Scripture, we see a unified revelation of Jesus: He is fully God, existing from eternity as the Logos, the source of life, and the one through whom creation itself came to be. He became flesh, entering our world as Jesus, both fully divine and fully human, to reveal God's heart to us and to fulfill His redemptive purpose. This broader view of Scripture allows us to see the fullness of who Jesus is—our eternal, unchanging Savior, and the complete revelation of God to humanity.

But thou, Bethlehem Ephratah, though thou be

little among the thousands of Judah, yet out of thee shall he come forth unto me that is to be ruler in Israel; whose goings forth have been from of old, from everlasting.
Micah 5:2 KJV

The prophet Micah's prediction of Jesus' birthplace is one of the Bible's profound testimonies to God's plan and power. Long before Jesus was born, Micah foretold that the Messiah would come from Bethlehem, a small town in Judah (Micah 5:2). But this prophecy wasn't just about a location; it revealed the extraordinary identity of the Messiah. Micah describes Him as one whose origins are "from of old, from ancient times"—a being from eternity. This points directly to Jesus' divine nature, as only God Himself can be everlasting.

In the Gospel of John, the eternal nature of Jesus is made even more clear. John 1:1-3 tells us that "In the beginning was the Word, and the Word was with God, and the Word was God." Here, John identifies Jesus as the eternal Logos, or Word, who was not only with God but was indeed God Himself. The text goes on to say that "all things were made through him, and without him, nothing was made that has been made." Jesus was actively involved in creation, showing His unity with the Father and His divine power.

God's ability to fulfill this incredible prophecy is a reminder of His limitless character. Just as God can make the impossible happen, He brought forth His Son in human form while remaining one with Him as the eternal God. Jesus' incarnation shows that He is both distinct in person and one with God in essence, something that surpasses human understanding. If we, as humans, can imagine concepts like a spirit leaving and returning to the body, how much more can our Creator accomplish what is beyond our limited comprehension?

The Bible challenges us to see God as the one who transcends all human limitations, working in ways that are far beyond our understanding. In Jesus, God made Himself known to us in a tangible way, yet His divine nature remains just as profound and boundless. Jesus, as the Word, is equal with God and remains so for all eternity. This truth calls us to trust in God's greatness and to acknowledge Jesus as the eternal Savior who reveals God's heart to humanity.

Let this mind be in you, which was also in Christ Jesus: Who, being in the form of God, thought it not robbery to be equal with God: But made himself of no reputation, and took on him the form of a servant, and was made in the likeness of men: And being found in fashion as a man, he humbled himself, and became obedient to death, even the death of the cross.
Philippians 2:5-8 KJV.

The Scriptures reveal Jesus as both fully God and fully man, a profound mystery at the heart of Christian belief. In the New Testament, we see Jesus described as the eternal Logos, or Word—John's term to capture Christ's unique divine nature and active role in creation (John 1:1-3). By calling Him the Word, John emphasizes that Jesus was not only with God in the beginning but was God Himself, sharing in the very essence and power of God. This underscores His deity and co-participation in the divine essence, spanning from eternity past to eternity future.

However, in His incarnation, Jesus willingly set aside the independent use of His divine attributes. As Paul writes in Philippians 2:6-8: "Though he was in the form of God, did not count equality with God something to be grasped, but emptied himself, by taking the form of a servant, being born in the likeness of men."

Here, "emptied himself" does not mean that Jesus ceased to be God; rather, He set aside His divine privileges and lived in complete submission to the Father's will. His purpose was not to assert His glory but to fulfill God's redemptive plan for humanity, even to the point of death on the cross. Jesus' choice to obey—even unto death—reflects His complete surrender to the Father, demonstrating what it means to be a true servant.

John clarifies that "the Word became flesh and dwelt among us" (John 1:14). This incarnation was not a departure from His divine identity but an addition to it. Jesus took on humanity while maintaining His divine nature, bridging the divide between God and humanity in a way that only He could. Through this, God revealed Himself intimately to us in Jesus. We see the glory of

God—not as a distant power but embodied in the life, love, and sacrifice of Christ.

The miracle of the incarnation shows us that Jesus is not just another figure or prophet. He is the Word who became flesh—the living revelation of God's love and holiness, walking among us. Through His earthly ministry, death, and resurrection, Jesus demonstrated both His divine authority and His complete identification with human suffering. As the one who is both God and man, Jesus stands alone in His power to redeem—bridging heaven and earth so that we, too, may share in God's eternal life.

And he was clothed with a vesture dipped in blood: and his name is called The Word of God. Revelation 19:13

C. Clifton Black's commentary on 1 John 1:1-2:2, provides a profound exploration into how John uses the concept of the Logos to reveal Jesus as the eternal Word. Black emphasizes that John's purpose in using the term "Logos" is to present Jesus not only as the one who was present at the beginning, but as the very embodiment of God's creative power, holiness, and redemptive grace. John's Gospel opens with the powerful assertion that "In the beginning was the Word, and the Word was with God, and the Word was God" (John 1:1), showing Jesus as the eternal presence who has always been with God and, in fact, is God.

By calling Jesus the Logos, John situates Christ as both the Creator and the ultimate revelation of God's nature, giving humanity a direct encounter with God through Him. This title also signifies the authority and power of Jesus, as the Word of God is not only creative, but also carries the weight of divine truth, judgment, and salvation. Black's insights draw attention to the way John develops a cohesive understanding of Jesus' identity, tracing the Logos from creation to the incarnation and, ultimately, to His role in judgment and redemption as depicted in Revelation 19:13. Here, John again refers to Jesus as the Word of God, a powerful name evoking His eternal role and authority, especially as He returns to complete God's work in history.

In using the Word to describe Jesus, John emphasizes that Jesus is the full revelation of God in the flesh—God's wisdom, love, and truth manifest. John's portrayal of Jesus as the Logos thus calls believers to see Him not as an abstract idea but as the living and active presence of God. In Jesus, we see the heart of God, made visible and accessible to us. This is the crux of John's message: that by knowing Jesus, humanity can truly know and be reconciled with God. Black's commentary clarifies how John's approach allowed the early church, and readers today, to understand the fullness of Christ's divine and human nature as the eternal, incarnate, and glorified Word.

First, John's opening plays a riff on the Fourth

Gospel's first verses. Notice their similar language:

the Word or "the word of life" that was "in" or "from the beginning" (John 1:1; 1 John 1:1)

a life made manifest and testified to (John 1:4, 7, 15; 1 John 1:2)

the intimacy of God the Father with his Son Jesus Christ (John 1:14, 17-18; 1 John 1:3)

the proclamation of the Word (John 1:4-5, 7-9) or of God (1 John 1:5) as light unquenched by darkness

In contrast, the distinctive contributions of 1 John 1:1-4 are to draw at least two things out of John's background and set them centre stage.

First, the Gospel highlights Christ's divine glory, assuming his incarnation (John 1:1-3, 14). 1 John reverses the polarity by repeatedly stressing the sensory character of "the eternal life that was with the Father and made manifest to us" (1 John 1:2): "what we have heard, what we have seen with our own eyes, and we have beheld and touched with our own hands" (1 John 1:1, 3).

Most of these verbs are conjugated in the perfect tense, which connotes a past reality extending into the reader's present. Right out of the starting gate, 1 John commends as truthful confession "Jesus Christ's coming in the flesh" (1 John 4:2) and repudiates any denial of the Son's genuine humanity (1 John 4:3).

1 John's other manifest concern is the importance of genuine fellowship (koinonia) "with us" and "with the Father and with his Son Jesus Christ" (1 John 1:3).

In simple terms, this is 1 John's theme throughout: the coherence of the church with God's love expressed in Jesus Christ. In practice, it is not at all simple; for soon we learn that the letter's author is distraught over a schism in that church, a divorce over who Jesus is and the difference his coming has made (cf. 1 John 2:18-25; 4:1-6; 5:1-12). The author writes with heartfelt hope that "our joy may be consummated" (1 John 1:4)

Finally, John talks about who bears witness of Jesus as the Word.

For there are three that bear record in heaven, the Father, the Word, and the Holy Ghost: and these three are one. And there are three that bear witness in earth, the Spirit, and the water, and the blood: and these three agree in one. If we receive the witness of men, the witness of God is greater: for this is the witness of God which he hath testified of his Son. He that believeth on the Son of God hath the witness in himself: he that believeth not God hath made him a liar, because he believeth not the record that God gave of his Son.

1 John 5: 6-9

John emphasizes the unique relationship between the Father and Jesus, portraying Jesus as the Son of God, who shares a close, eternal bond with the Father. The Father, as the "first Person," speaks to His divine authority and His relationship with the Son within the Trinity. John reinforces this by including moments where God explicitly confirms Jesus' identity and mission as His Son.

In Matthew 3:16-17, during Jesus' baptism, God publicly identifies Jesus as His beloved Son, with the Spirit descending upon Him in the form of a dove, visually symbolizing the unity of the Father, Son, and Holy Spirit. God's voice from heaven declares, "This is my beloved Son, with whom I am well pleased," showing that Jesus carries the Father's full approval and authority.

Similarly, at the transfiguration in Matthew 17:5, God speaks once more, affirming Jesus' sonship and commanding the disciples to "Listen to Him!" Here, Jesus is again revealed as the unique, beloved Son, now in a glorified state, providing a glimpse of His divine glory.

These passages confirm Jesus' sonship and divinity, indicating that the Father Himself bears witness to Jesus' identity, establishing that Jesus is not merely a prophet or teacher but the divine Son of God. Through these affirmations, John and the Gospels invite readers to recognize Jesus as the direct revelation of God, the one in whom the fullness of God dwells, and who has the authority to reveal the Father to humanity.

In John's writings, "the Word" refers to Jesus as the second Person of the Trinity, existing eternally with God and as God. This title emphasizes Jesus' divine role in creation—He is the one through whom all things were made. John reveals that Jesus is not a created being but is co-eternal with the Father, the agent of creation, and an essential part of the divine nature. This idea is reinforced in John 1:1, "In the beginning was the Word, and the Word was with God, and the Word was God," affirming His deity and distinct personhood within the Trinity.

John the Baptist recognizes Jesus as "the Lamb of God," symbolizing the one who would take away the sins of the world through His sacrificial death. This title points to Jesus' role in God's plan of salvation, fulfilling the sacrificial system and foreshadowing His atoning death on the cross. Meanwhile, Peter's confession of Jesus as "the Son of the living God" (Matthew 16:16) testifies to Jesus' divine identity and mission. Peter's declaration acknowledges Jesus as more than a prophet or teacher; He is the divine Son, sent by God to redeem humanity.

The Holy Spirit, described as the third Person of the Trinity, testifies to Christ's identity at Jesus' baptism. When He descends like a dove, the Spirit confirms Jesus' sonship and anoints Him for His earthly ministry, showing the unity and distinct roles of the Father, Son, and Holy Spirit.

Together, these accounts—John's declaration of the Word, John the Baptist's recognition of the Lamb of God, Peter's confession, and the Spirit's descent—build a complete picture of Jesus' identity. John underscores that Jesus is indeed the Word, existing eternally with God, fully divine, and the one through whom God reveals Himself to humanity.

Take a look at this passage from the book "A New Systematic Theology of the Christian Faith":

[The eternal Word] subjected himself to birth for us, and came forth man from a woman, without casting off that which he was .... Although he assumed flesh and blood, he remained what he was, God in essence and in truth. Neither do we say that his flesh was changed into the nature of divinity, nor that the ineffable nature of the Word of God was for the nature of the flesh; for he is unchanged and absolutely unchangeable, being the same always, according to the scriptures. For although visible and a child in swaddling clothes, and even in the bosom of his virgin mother, he filled all creation as God and was a fellow-ruler with him who begot him, for the Godhead is without quantity and dimension, and cannot have limits.

What a profound truth! Jesus Christ, who entered the world through His birth of a woman, is the eternal Word, coexistent with God from the beginning. As Philippians 2:6 states, "Who, being in very nature God, did not consider equality with God something to be used to his own advantage." This verse emphasizes His divine nature and His humility in taking on human form.

Christ's incarnation did not diminish His deity. Instead, it revealed His divine nature in a way humanity could see and understand. As John 1:14 declares, "The Word became flesh and made his dwelling among us. We have seen his glory, the glory of the one and only Son, who came from the Father, full of grace and truth." Jesus became the living embodiment of God's Word—a perfect example of God's love, truth, and righteousness.

By stepping into our world, Jesus bridged the gap between humanity and God. He did not cease to be God; rather, He added humanity to His divinity, becoming fully God and fully man. This mystery of the incarnation demonstrates His love and willingness to humble Himself for our salvation.

His life on earth was a living testimony of the Word itself—His teachings, actions, and ultimate sacrifice all pointed back to the eternal truth of God. He not only taught us how to live but also showed us, through His life, the character and will of God. Through Christ, we see the fullness of God's grace and truth revealed in a tangible, relatable way.

Jesus' incarnation is the cornerstone of our faith, showing that God is not distant or detached but intimately involved in our redemption. He took on flesh to save us, to fulfill the promises of God, and to invite us into eternal relationship with Him. What an incredible act of love and humility!

What does John mean by "the Word"? the Word was a term used by theologians and philosophers, both Jews and Greeks, in many different ways. In Hebrews Scripture, the Word was an agent of creation (Psalm 33:6), the source of God's message to this people through the prophets (Hosea 4:1) and God's law, his standard of holiness (Psalm 119:11)in Greek philosophy, the Word was the principle of reason that governed the world, or the though still in the mind, while in Hebrew though, the Word was another expression for God. John's description shows clearly that he is speaking of Jesus (see especially 1:14) – a human being he knew and love, but at the same time the creator of the universe, the ultimate revelation of God. The living picture of God's holiness, the one who "holds all creation together" (Colossians 1:17). To Jewish readers, to say this man Jesus "was God" was blasphemous. To Greek readers, "the Word became human" (1:14) was unthinkable. To John, this new understanding of the Word was the Good News of Jesus Christ.

Again, Jesus as the Logos (the "Word") is a profound concept that communicates both His divinity and His unique role in relation to God the Father. In John 1:1-3, the Logos is presented as being with God from the very beginning and as God Himself. This reveals Jesus as eternally co-existent with the Father, distinct in person yet fully divine. This mystery of the Trinity shows that Jesus shares the same divine essence as the Father and the Holy Spirit, while remaining a distinct person within the Godhead.

Colossians 1:15-17 speaks of Jesus as "the image of the invisible God," making Him the visible representation of God to humanity. Where God the Father is spirit and unseen, Jesus embodies God in physical form, bridging the divide between the divine and human realms. As Hebrews 1:1-3 emphasizes, Jesus is "the radiance of God's glory and the exact representation of His being," affirming His deity while still being distinct from the Father. This passage also tells us that it is through Jesus, the Logos, that the world was created, upheld, and sustained.

In Genesis 1, we see God speaking creation into existence through His Word. This spoken Word is not just sound or command but is embodied in the Logos, the eternal Son who carries out the creative will of the Father. In this way, the universe was brought into being by God speaking through the Word—Jesus as the active agent of creation. In the fullness of time, this same Word took on flesh (John 1:14), becoming human to dwell among us, revealing God in the most tangible and relatable way.

Thus, Jesus was, is, and always will be the Logos —the eternal Word who is God, yet distinct in His relationship with the Father, and now made flesh as Jesus the Christ. His existence embodies God's nature, power, and presence, making Him the centre of God's revelation to humanity. This truth is the heart of the Christian understanding of Jesus: God Himself, who came to us in a form we could understand, love, and follow.

CHAPTER TWO
JESUS THE ROCK

Calling Jesus, the "Rock in a weary land" is a powerful way of recognizing Him as a source of strength, stability, and provision, especially in times of hardship. In the Old Testament, Israel's encounter with the rock in the wilderness underscores this symbolism: as they journeyed through a barren desert, God miraculously provided life-sustaining water from a rock (Exodus 17:6; Numbers 20:8-11). This physical rock became a profound emblem of God's ability to care for and sustain His people, even in the bleakest circumstances.

The Apostle Paul further explains this connection in 1 Corinthians 10:4, where he refers to the rock that provided water as a symbol of Christ Himself: "for they drank from the spiritual rock that accompanied them, and that rock was Christ." In this way, Jesus is seen as the true Rock—one who offers sustenance, strength, and life to those in a spiritually barren world. Just as the rock in the wilderness was the means by which Israel's thirst was quenched, Jesus, the living water, satisfies our deepest spiritual thirst.

This metaphor speaks to Jesus' unchanging nature and His reliability as a refuge. No matter how desolate or wearying life becomes, He remains steadfast, providing renewal and strength. Just as the rock in the wilderness symbolized God's provision and presence with Israel, Jesus is our "Rock" who promises never to leave or forsake us, continually offering us sustenance, hope, and spiritual life.

Jesus as the "Source of Life and Sustenance" connects deeply to the idea of Him as our living water, which meets our spiritual needs in ways nothing else can. In John 4:14, Jesus tells the Samaritan woman that whoever drinks the water He gives will never thirst again, signifying a continuous, all-sufficient source of spiritual life that satisfies the deepest needs of the human soul. Just as water flowed from the rock to quench Israel's physical thirst in the wilderness, Jesus provides life-giving, eternal sustenance for our spirits.

The image of Jesus as our "Stability and Foundation" emphasizes His role as the unshakable base upon which we can build our lives. In Matthew 7:24-25, He describes the strength of a life built on His teachings, comparing it to a house set on a rock that remains solid even when storms hit. This analogy reflects Jesus' enduring strength and reliability, suggesting that in trusting and following Him, we have a foundation that can withstand any challenges or hardships.

Together, these two aspects—Jesus as the Living Water and as the Rock—reflect His role as both the essential source of life and the unmovable ground upon which we find stability. He is both our sustenance in times of spiritual need and our steady, enduring foundation amidst life's storms.

The image of Jesus as our "Protection and Refuge" resonates powerfully with the biblical tradition of God as a safe haven for His people. In times of danger or distress, ancient travellers and soldiers would seek shelter in caves or rock formations, finding physical protection in their unyielding strength. Psalm 18:2 captures this beautifully, calling the Lord "my rock, my fortress, and my deliverer," a place of safety that stands strong and secure when all else may fail. Just as these rock formations provided physical protection, Jesus offers a spiritual refuge, a place of unwavering safety for those who turn to Him in faith.

When we speak of Jesus as the "Rock in a weary land," we are reminded that, like Israel wandering through the wilderness, we too can rely on Him for all we need. Jesus provides us with sustenance through the "living water" that quenches our spiritual thirst. He offers us stability, standing as our firm foundation when we face life's uncertainties. And He is our protector, a refuge to whom we can cling when life feels overwhelming.

In Jesus, we find not only physical and spiritual provision but also the assurance of eternal security. His presence comforts, strengthens, and sustains us through the weariness of this world, leading us toward the promise of eternal life in His care.

Moreover, brethren, I would not that ye should be ignorant, how that all our fathers were under the cloud, and all passed through the sea; And were all baptized unto Moses in the cloud and in the sea; And did all eat the same spiritual meat; And did all drink the same spiritual drink: for they drank of that spiritual Rock that followed them: and that Rock was Christ. 1 Corinthians 10:1-4

Paul's message to the Corinthians in 1 Corinthians 10:1-13 is a powerful reminder that spiritual experiences and blessings, while valuable, do not automatically result in a faithful or righteous life. By drawing parallels between Israel's experiences in the wilderness and the sacraments of baptism and the Lord's Supper, Paul cautions believers against a misplaced reliance on rituals alone for salvation.

In the wilderness, Israel was privileged to experience God's direct guidance and provision. They were "baptized into Moses in the cloud and in the sea," symbolizing their deliverance and union with God through Moses as they passed through the Red Sea. Similarly, their consumption of "spiritual food and drink"—the manna and the water from the rock—prefigured the sustenance that Christ would later offer as the "Bread of Life" and the "Living Water." These moments were foreshadowing of the Christian ordinances of baptism and the Eucharist, which signify spiritual union with Christ and the reception of His life-giving grace.

However, Paul points out that despite these blessings, many in Israel failed to remain faithful, fell into sin, and faced God's judgment. This serves as a warning to the Corinthians (and all believers) that merely participating in sacred practices is insufficient if one's heart is not genuinely aligned with God. Just as Israel's privileges did not shield them from the consequences of idolatry and immorality, neither does baptism or the Lord's Supper exempt Christians from the need for true repentance, obedience, and accountability.

By examining Israel's mistakes, Paul urges believers to remain vigilant, grounded in humility and self-examination, understanding that spiritual privileges come with responsibilities. His message underscores that a life of genuine faith involves more than outward signs; it requires a continual commitment to walking in righteousness, guided by the transformative power of Christ's Spirit. Through this teaching, Paul encourages believers to use the experiences of Israel as a cautionary tale—reminding them that faith and obedience are foundational to the Christian journey.

Paul's message to the Corinthians invites deep reflection on several key points:

Ordinances as Symbols, Not Guarantees of Salvation: Paul's warning to the Corinthians emphasizes that while ordinances like baptism and the Lord's Supper are central to the Christian faith, they are not guarantees of salvation on their own. Israel's experiences in 1 Corinthians 10:1-5, serve as a powerful illustration—though they participated in a form of "baptism" through the Red Sea and received spiritual nourishment from manna and water, these privileges did not exempt them from judgment when they disobeyed. This teaches us that mere outward participation in sacred acts, without genuine faith and a life committed to God, cannot lead to salvation. True faith is marked by obedience, humility, and repentance, underscoring that transformation must be internal as well as external.

Christ as the Rock and the Spiritual Provision: Paul's identification of Christ as the Rock that provided water in the wilderness highlights Jesus as the ultimate source of spiritual sustenance. The water that flowed from the rock, struck by Moses, prefigures Christ's sacrificial death on the cross.

What a beautiful and theologically rich connection! The imagery of life-giving water flowing from the smitten rock in Exodus 17:6 profoundly foreshadows the salvation offered through Christ. When

Moses struck the rock at God's command, water gushed out to quench the thirst of the Israelites, sustaining them in the wilderness. This miraculous provision points directly to Christ, who was "struck" on the cross for our sins, becoming the source of spiritual life and eternal salvation.

Paul draws this connection explicitly in 1 Corinthians 10:4: "They drank from the spiritual rock that accompanied them, and that rock was Christ." This parallel reveal that just as the rock in the wilderness gave physical sustenance, Christ, the spiritual Rock, offers living water—eternal life and the forgiveness of sins.

Hebrews 9:22 reminds us that "without the shedding of blood, there is no forgiveness." Jesus' sacrifice was necessary to open the way for humanity to be reconciled to God. His crucifixion was the ultimate act of love and obedience, and through it, the floodgates of grace and mercy were opened for all who believe. Just as the water from the rock was freely given to the Israelites, so too is the gift of salvation freely offered to anyone who comes to Christ in faith.

This imagery also emphasizes Christ's sufficiency. The rock in the wilderness provided all the water the Israelites needed, just as Christ provides everything, we need for spiritual life. In John 7:37-38, Jesus says, "If anyone is thirsty, let him come to me and drink. Whoever believes in me, as Scripture has said, rivers of living water will flow from within them."

Through Him, we are not only forgiven but also filled with the Holy Spirit, empowered to live in relationship with God and to share His life-giving truth with others.

Christ as the smitten Rock is not just a symbol; it's a vital truth of the Gospel. His sacrifice is the foundation of our faith and the source of our eternal hope. Without it, there would be no salvation. Yet, through His death and resurrection, we are given access to the life-giving waters of grace, love, and redemption—waters that will never run dry.

A Call to Faithfulness and Obedience: By reminding the Corinthians of Israel's failures despite their blessings, Paul encourages a life of vigilance and faithfulness. He warns against complacency, calling believers to take seriously the call to holiness and to walk in obedience. This message cautions against presuming on God's grace and teaches those privileges like church membership, participation in the sacraments, and knowledge of Scripture should lead us closer to God and deepen our walk with Him, not become substitutes for a life marked by integrity and obedience.

In summary, Paul's teaching in 1 Corinthians 10 serves as a reminder that true faith is evidenced by a transformed life. While the ordinances are sacred and powerful, they must be accompanied by a heart surrendered to Christ, nourished by His Spirit, and committed to walking in His ways. The example of Israel challenges us to examine our own hearts and live in a way that honours the sacrificial love of Christ, our Rock, and Redeemer.

The imagery of the smitten rock in the wilderness as a foreshadowing of Christ's sacrifice is rich with meaning. In Exodus 17:6, when God instructed Moses to strike the rock, the resulting flow of water was not just a miraculous provision for physical thirst but also a prophetic symbol of the life-giving salvation to come through Christ. Just as water flowed to sustain the Israelites, so too does spiritual life flow from Christ's crucifixion, where He was "struck" for our sins. His sacrifice offers living water—eternal life—to all who believe (John 4:14). This parallel emphasizes that Christ's suffering was the source from which God's grace and salvation flow, sustaining us in our spiritual journey much as the water sustained Israel.

Paul's warning to the Corinthians expands on this by cautioning them not to take God's grace lightly. Just as the Israelites experienced God's miraculous provision yet later fell into sin, Christians, too, must be vigilant. Holy ordinances like baptism and the Lord's Supper are profound symbols of our faith and participation in Christ's sacrifice, but Paul underscores that these alone are not sufficient without true faith and a life marked by holiness.

The sacraments serve as powerful means of grace, reminding us of Christ's work and deepening our connection with Him. However, they also call us to self-examination and commitment. The Israelites' failures in the wilderness serve as a reminder that spiritual blessings and participation in holy acts do not exempt anyone from accountability. Just as the Corinthians were reminded, we, too, are called to live in a way that reflects gratitude for Christ's sacrifice, avoiding complacency and embracing a lifestyle of repentance, faith, and holiness.

Through this, Paul's message resounds with timeless relevance: Christ, the smitten Rock, offers life to all who draw near in faith, yet this gift calls us to a life committed to following Him in truth and humility.

Paul's message, emphasizing the need for inward transformation and true obedience, reminds believers that outward observance of rituals without sincere commitment and obedience is insufficient. He draws on Israel's history in the wilderness to demonstrate that privilege and divine provision do not excuse sin. Just as Israel received blessings yet often fell into disobedience and suffered the consequences, believers are called to hold fast to Christ, the true Rock, in both faith and obedience.

Isaiah 53 is one of the most poignant and prophetic passages in Scripture, painting a vivid picture of the suffering Messiah who would redeem humanity. The verse "Surely he has borne our griefs and carried our sorrows" (Isaiah 53:4) captures the profound reality of Christ's sacrificial love. This prophecy reveals a Savior who would take upon Himself the weight of our sins, griefs, and sorrows, embodying God's plan for redemption through His suffering.

The phrase "smitten by God" (Isaiah 53:4) highlights the divine purpose and intentionality behind Jesus' crucifixion. It underscores that His suffering was not accidental, but a fulfilment of God's redemptive plan. On the cross, Jesus bore the wrath and judgment for sin that we deserved. As 2 Corinthians 5:21 explains, "God made him who had no sin to be sin for us, so that in him we might become the righteousness of God."

This imagery ties powerfully to the account of the rock in the wilderness. When Moses struck the rock at God's command, it released life-giving water for the Israelites (Exodus 17:6). Similarly, Jesus, the true and eternal Rock, was struck through His crucifixion, releasing spiritual life for all who believe in Him. The connection between the "smitten" rock and the "smitten" Messiah reinforces the truth that through Christ's sacrifice, we receive the living water of salvation, as Jesus declared in John 7:37-38: "If anyone thirsts, let him come to me and drink."

Isaiah's prophecy also highlights the personal cost of redemption. Jesus was "wounded for our transgressions" and "bruised for our iniquities," with the chastisement for our peace laid upon Him (Isaiah 53:5). This profound act of substitutionary atonement shows the depth of God's love for humanity, as Christ endured the suffering and punishment that we might be reconciled to God.

The parallels between Isaiah's prophecy and the striking of the rock in the wilderness, illuminate the heart of the Gospel: Jesus, the suffering Servant and the smitten Rock, bore our sins and griefs so that we could receive forgiveness, healing, and eternal life. Through His sacrifice, the spiritual thirst of humanity is quenched, and we are invited into a restored relationship with God—a relationship made possible only through the life-giving work of the Messiah.

1 Samuel 15:22 stands as a powerful reminder of the priority God places on obedience over outward rituals. When Samuel confronts Saul, he highlights that God is not primarily interested in the external act of sacrifice but in the internal posture of the heart: "Does the Lord delight in burnt offerings and sacrifices as much as in obeying the Lord? To obey is better than sacrifice, and to heed is better than the fat of rams." This declaration underscores that true worship begins with a heart fully surrendered to God's will.

Samuel's message directly addresses the tendency to substitute outward religious acts for genuine faith and obedience. Saul had disobeyed God's clear command, attempting to justify his actions with the offering of sacrifices. But Samuel's rebuke reveals that no ritual, however costly, can replace the fundamental requirement of obedience to God's Word.

This truth aligns with Paul's teaching to the

Corinthians, where he cautions against prioritizing ritual over a sincere heart. Paul frequently reminds his readers that actions, even good ones, are meaningless without the right motivation. In 1 Corinthians 13:3, he states, "If I give all I possess to the poor and give over my body to hardship that I may boast, but do not have love, I gain nothing." Obedience, grounded in love and faith, is the foundation of a life that pleases God.

God's desire is for a relationship with His people, not empty gestures or legalistic adherence to rituals. This theme is echoed throughout Scripture. In Hosea 6:6, God declares, "For I desire mercy, not sacrifice, and acknowledgment of God rather than burnt offerings." Jesus Himself reiterates this principle in Matthew 9:13 and Matthew 12:7, emphasizing that God values a heart devoted to Him above religious observances.

Sacrifices and rituals are not inherently wrong; they were given by God as expressions of worship and reminders of His holiness. However, when they are performed without faith, repentance, or obedience, they become hollow and even offensive to God (Isaiah 1:11-17). True worship flows from a heart aligned with God's will, marked by humility, faith, and a desire to follow His commands.

Samuel's declaration challenges us to examine our own lives. Are we simply going through the motions of religion, or are we walking in genuine obedience to God? His words remind us of that what God seeks is not a performance, but a relationship—a life that reflects His love, grace, and truth through faithful obedience.

Deuteronomy 32, often called the "Song of Moses," is a sobering and poetic reminder of God's faithfulness contrasted with Israel's repeated rebellion. It recounts God's provision, mercy, and justice, while also serving as a warning of the dire consequences of turning away from Him. Moses' song is both a historical reflection and a prophetic message, urging Israel to remain faithful and to recognize the gravity of disobedience in Deuteronomy 32:15: "They abandoned the God who made them and rejected the Rock their Savior."

The song highlights the tension between God's steadfast love and His righteous judgment. Despite His continual provision and protection—described as an eagle caring for its young (Deuteronomy 32:11)—Israel often turned to idolatry and rebellion. The consequences of such actions, including divine discipline, are laid out not as a desire to destroy but to call Israel back to covenant faithfulness.

Paul echoes these warnings in 1 Corinthians 10:1-11, drawing from Israel's history as an example for New Testament believers. He writes in 1 Corinthians 10:11, "These things happened to them as examples and were written down as warnings for us." Paul reminds the Corinthians that although the Israelites experienced God's miraculous deliverance and provision, many still fell under judgment because of their disobedience. Their rebellion, particularly in idolatry and moral compromise, serves as a cautionary tale to not take God's grace for granted.

This warning resonates with all believers. As members of the faith community, it's easy to presume upon God's grace, thinking that proximity to His blessings or participation in religious practices ensures security. However, both Moses' song and Paul's admonition emphasize that rebellion—whether through neglect of God's commands, idolatry, or moral compromise—alienates us from His fellowship and invites discipline.

The underlying message is not merely about fear of consequences, but about the call to fidelity and gratitude. God's mercy and provision should inspire reverence and obedience, not complacency. As Moses declares in Deuteronomy 32:4, "He is the Rock, his works are perfect, and all his ways are just." Recognizing God's character and faithfulness motivates us to align our lives with His will, avoiding the pitfalls of rebellion and instead living in covenant relationship with Him.

The gravity of disobedience lies in the fact that it disrupts our relationship with God and undermines His purposes for us. Yet, even in judgment, God's ultimate goal is restoration. Both Deuteronomy 32 and Paul's writings remind us of His enduring desire for His people to repent and return to Him. They serve as a timeless call to humility, faithfulness, and a deeper understanding of the grace we have received.

Beautifully stated! The overarching narrative of Scripture demonstrates that God's plan of salvation is a harmonious blend of obedience, sacrifice, and grace, culminating in Jesus Christ. Through the prophetic imagery of Isaiah 53, we see the suffering servant who bears the weight of humanity's sin, offering Himself as the ultimate sacrifice to bring life and restoration to a broken world. Jesus, the "smitten" Messiah, fulfills the role of the sacrificial Lamb and the life-giving Rock, showing that salvation is entirely God's initiative, yet it requires a response from us.

Paul's exhortations to the early church reinforce this truth: Salvation is not a passive gift but one that calls believers to an active response of faith and obedience. As he writes in Philippians 2:12, "continue to work out your salvation with fear and trembling," Paul emphasizes that while salvation is secured by grace alone, it demands a life marked by reverence and devotion. Faith without works—without a transformed life—is incomplete (James 2:17).

The example of Israel in the wilderness serves as a timeless warning and encouragement. Despite experiencing God's miraculous provision and deliverance, their disobedience led to judgment. Their story reminds believers today of the importance of aligning their lives with God's will, trusting in His promises, and living in light of Christ's sacrifice.

This call to alignment is not about earning salvation, but about living in gratitude for it. As Ephesians 2:8-10 explains, we are saved by grace through faith, not by works, yet we are created in Christ Jesus "to do good works, which God prepared in advance for us to do." True faith produces obedience, and genuine devotion flows from understanding the depth of Christ's sacrifice.

These passages collectively highlight the profound truth that salvation is both a gift and a calling. It begins and ends with grace—grace that provides the way of redemption, sustains us in our journey, and empowers us to live faithfully. As believers, we are invited to respond to this grace by surrendering our lives, walking in obedience, and reflecting the love and holiness of the God who has redeemed us. In this way, we honour the sacrifice of Christ, allowing His life, death, and resurrection to shape every aspect of our journey with Him.

Key Insights from our Reflection:
The Importance of Obedience (1 Samuel 15:22):
Obedience is more valuable than sacrifice in God's eyes. Samuel's words to King Saul serve as a reminder that God desires true, heart-driven obedience, not just external acts of ritual. The Bible emphasizes that obedience to God's commands reveals a deeper

relationship with Him, rooted in trust and humility. Sacrifices and offerings, though important, are meaningless if they are not backed by a genuine and obedient heart.

The Significance of Moses' Disobedience (Numbers 20:7-12):

Moses' failure to follow God's instructions in striking the rock instead of speaking to it may have seemed like a small act, but it was symbolic of a deeper heart issue. His act of disobedience stemmed from frustration, pride, and a lack of trust in God's ability to provide. This failure serves as a reminder that even small deviations from God's commands can have significant consequences. Moses' disobedience not only affected his ability to enter the Promised Land but also caused the people of Israel to miss out on experiencing the fullness of God's blessings.

The Posture of the Heart Matters (Matthew 15:8-9):

The central message is that God values the posture of our hearts. He desires hearts that are fully submitted to Him, characterized by trust, humility, and genuine love. Outward acts of worship or rituals are not enough if they are not accompanied by a heart of obedience. As Jesus teaches in Matthew 15, people can honour God with their lips, but if their hearts are far from Him, their worship is in vain. True relationship with God is defined by our willingness to obey His will, not by outward appearances.

Obedience and the Fulfilment of God's Promises (Deuteronomy 32:46-47):

Israel's history is filled with moments when disobedience led to judgment and the failure to enter into God's promises. Similarly, Paul urges the Corinthians to take seriously their relationship with God and to respond to His grace with faith and obedience. The journey through the wilderness and Israel's failure to trust God in moments of testing, parallels the Christian life: obedience to God's commands is essential in experiencing the fullness of His promises. Disobedience may lead to missed opportunities, but obedience positions us to receive God's blessing and fulfill His purpose for our lives.

Reflection for Our Lives:

The story of Moses and the Israelites challenges us to examine our own hearts and actions. Are we prioritizing outward actions while neglecting true obedience to God's commands? Do we trust God enough to follow His instructions, even when they seem difficult or unclear? In the Christian life, it is not just about participating in rituals or outward acts of worship but about cultivating a heart that is willing to obey and trust in God's perfect plan.

By focusing on obedience, humility, and trust, we can live in a way that honours God and positions us to receive His blessings and promises.

Human Tendency to Turn Away from God (Deuteronomy 32)

In Deuteronomy 32, also known as the Song of Moses, we see a poignant reflection of both God's faithfulness and Israel's repeated unfaithfulness. The chapter serves as a reminder of God's unchanging nature, righteousness, and perfection, symbolized by the metaphor of God as the Rock (v. 4). Despite this, Israel repeatedly forsakes God, their Rock and Savior, turning to idolatry and rebellion. This song foreshadows a recurrent theme in Scripture: the tendency of human beings to forget God's greatness, turn away from His ways, and follow their own desires.

Key Insights:
The Rock of Salvation

God is consistently portrayed as the Rock—a symbol of stability, strength, and unchanging faithfulness. However, in verse 15, Israel, "forsook God who made them and lightly esteemed the Rock of their salvation." This speaks to the human tendency to become complacent or proud, thinking we no longer need God, and failing to give Him the reverence and devotion He deserves. This is a warning to all believers: even after experiencing God's goodness, we can easily drift away if we aren't careful to stay humble and dependent on Him.

The Temptation of Idolatry and Self-Reliance

In verse 17, Israel turns to idol worship, sacrificing to "devils and not to God." This shift from worshiping the true God to following idols is symbolic of what happens when we allow our hearts to stray from God. We begin to elevate things that give us immediate gratification or power, instead of trusting in God's sovereignty. The root of idolatry often stems from pride —the desire to control our own destiny and act as though we are in control of our own lives. Similarly, when we prioritize self-reliance, we forsake God's provision, making ourselves our own gods.

Consequences of Forsaking God

Both in Moses' life and in Israel's history, we see that turning away from God comes with consequences. Moses' disobedience caused him to be excluded from the Promised Land (Numbers 20:12). Israel, too, faced the divine judgment of exile, suffering, and loss of God's blessings. The root cause of Israel's rebellion is often pride—they thought they could handle things on their own, or they trusted in other gods. This spiritual pride led them to forsake the One who had been their Rock and Sustainer.

Corruption and Judgment

The Song of Moses highlights that when people forsake God, they corrupt themselves (v. 5). Disobedience leads to spiritual and moral decay, and we invite divine judgment. Ignoring God's authority, His providence, and His salvation leads to corruption, both personally and collectively. Israel's failure to recognize and submit to God's authority resulted in their spiritual downfall, and the same applies to individuals or nations today.

The Deeper Lessons:

Human Nature and the Need for Vigilance: Moses' song is not just a historical recount but also a reflection on human nature. It shows how easy it is to turn away from God, even after experiencing His blessings. The key message is to remain vigilant and not take God's goodness for granted. We must regularly examine our hearts and ask: Are we relying on God or becoming self-sufficient in our own eyes?

Pride and Rebellion: The connection between pride and rebellion is key. Pride leads us to act out of our own wisdom and self-reliance, which often leads to spiritual downfall. Rebellion, in this context, is not just about outwardly defying God, but also about an internal posture of independence—thinking that we know better than God and not trusting His plan.

The Danger of Idolatry: Idolatry can take many forms in modern life—materialism, self-idolatry, pleasure-seeking, ambition—things that we elevate to the status of "gods" when we rely on them more than we rely on God. This is a direct consequence of forsaking our relationship with the Rock who provides for us, sustains us, and calls us to obedience.

God's Faithfulness and Justice: Even as Israel turned away, God remained faithful, reminding them of His unchanging nature and perfect justice. His judgments were not arbitrary but were always tied to His perfect righteousness. When we turn away from God, we can expect consequences, but God also offers mercy to those who repent and return to Him.

Conclusion:

The Song of Moses in Deuteronomy 32 is a poignant reminder of both the greatness of God and the human tendency to forsake Him. It challenges believers to recognize that obedience is not just about rituals, but about the heart posture of humility and trust in God. The chapter serves as a warning that pride, idolatry, and self-reliance will inevitably lead to spiritual decay and divine judgment, but when we return to God and recognize Him as our Rock, we can experience His faithfulness, provision, and salvation.

The Temptation to Self-Governance

The temptation to self-governance—the desire to live independently from God and act as our own authority—is a recurring theme throughout human history and the biblical narrative. From the very beginning, in Genesis 3, when Adam and Eve sought to determine good and evil for themselves, to the rebellion at Babel (Genesis 11), humanity has constantly tried to live apart from God's direction. This self-reliance reflects the heart of sin: the belief that we know better than God, and that we can govern our own lives without needing His guidance.

The root of this issue is the same throughout history: the desire for autonomy. We see this in the Garden of Eden, where Adam and Eve, though created in perfect harmony with God, wanted to be like Him by determining for themselves what is right and wrong. This is echoed later in Israel's history when, despite the extraordinary acts of God on their behalf, they still sought after idols and rebelled against His authority.

This autonomous mindset continues today—people often trust in their own wisdom, resources, and strength, relying on their understanding of the world rather than on God's Word. The self-sufficiency many pursue today leads them to idolatry, whether through the worship of possessions, status, or even self. Idolatry, in its broadest sense, is not just bowing down to statues but elevating anything—whether desires, ambitions, or even one another—above God's place in our lives. When we do this, we sin—missing the mark of God's righteousness.

The Call in Deuteronomy 32: Remembering God's Greatness

Deuteronomy 32 serves as a powerful reminder to the people of Israel—and to believers today—to remember God's greatness, provision, and steadfastness. Israel was repeatedly tempted to forget these truths and to trust in their own strength or in other gods. God, through Moses, calls them to remember that He is their Rock, their firm foundation in a weary land. Without recognizing Him as such, they were susceptible to the temptation of self-governance—acting on their own without God's guidance.

In verse 15, Moses laments how Israel, despite all of God's blessings, "forsook God who made them and lightly esteemed the Rock of their salvation." This was a tragic spiritual error. When they turned away from God, they fell into idolatry—the worship of false gods and their own desires.

The deeper lesson here is that when we turn away from God—whether through pride, self-reliance, or the pursuit of worldly desires—we end up creating idols. These idols take God's place in our lives, whether it is our ego, career, pleasure, or even the desire to control our circumstances. Just like Israel, we may trust in false securities and forget the true source of our life and salvation.

The Need for Constant Humility and Dependence on God

The failure of Moses—even though he was a great leader of God's people—further reinforces this truth. Moses, in his frustration and pride, disobeyed God by striking the rock instead of speaking to it, as God commanded. This act wasn't just about the physical action; it was a spiritual issue—Moses took matters into his own hands rather than obeying God's specific command. This demonstrates that even the most faithful and revered servants of God must constantly remain humble, trust in His instructions, and submit to His will.

The lesson from Moses' disobedience is profound: no one is above God's law. Even the greatest of leaders are held to the same standards of obedience and trust as everyone else. It's not about how much we know or how much we have done for God; it's about our relationship with Him and our willingness to obey.

When we fail to obey, just as Israel did, we risk falling into the same traps: pride, idolatry, and separation from God's blessings. Moses' failure to act as commanded led to a loss—he was denied entry into the Promised Land. In the same way, when we act outside of God's commands, we forfeit the fullness of His blessings in our lives.

Repentance: The Path Back

The path back to God is through repentance—a turning away from self-reliance, pride, and idolatry, and a return to humility, obedience, and submission to God's will. God is always willing to receive those who acknowledge their sin and turn to Him in faith.

In the case of Israel, after many cycles of rebellion and repentance, God continually offered them forgiveness and restoration when they repented. In the same way, Jesus offers grace and redemption for those who have wandered from God, but it requires us to humble ourselves and submit to His Lordship.

Conclusion: The True Source of Salvation, Provision, and Life

Ultimately, as we reflect on the temptation of self-governance and the call to humble submission, we are reminded that God is our true source of salvation, provision, and life. Idols—whether they are physical objects or our own pride—lead to destruction. But when we humble ourselves, recognize God as our Rock, and rely on His grace, we experience the fullness of His blessings.

Just as Moses was held accountable to God's word, so are we. As believers, we must resist the temptation to act autonomously and remember that true life and fulfilment come only through complete dependence on God, obedience to His word, and submission to His will.

Of the Rock that begat you, you are unmindful, and have forgotten God that formed you. Deuteronomy 32:18 KJV

The Consequences of Forgetting God

The ultimate failure of Israel was not just their failure to remember but their decision to forget the God of their salvation. This forgetfulness led to rebellion, idolatry, and ultimately their downfall. In the same way, believers today are warned against the danger of forgetting the salvation Christ has provided and acting as if they no longer need Him or His guidance.

Christ, the Rock, has provided the living water that sustains us spiritually. When we neglect or forget this provision, we too are in danger of rebellion and the loss of God's blessings. The call to remember God's faithfulness and His command to live in obedience remains central to our walk with Him.

Conclusion: Returning to the Rock

The journey through the wilderness—both for Israel and for us—serves as a reminder that God is the Rock who provides, sustains, and guides. We must keep His commandments and never forget the greatness of His works. Just as Israel was warned to remember God in their day of prosperity, so we are called to never forget the Christ, the Rock, who sustains us and who is the source of our salvation.

Obedience, humility, and repentance are the keys to returning to the fullness of God's grace and blessings. May we never forget the Rock that is our salvation and live in constant remembrance of His goodness, that we might always walk in His ways and experience His life-giving provision.

Yea, they spake against God; they said, Can God furnish a table in the wilderness? Behold, he smote the rock, that the waters gushed out, and the streams overflowed; can he give bread also? can he provide flesh for his people? Psalm 78: 19-20 KJV.

Israel's Ungratefulness: The Manna and the Rock

The Israelites' attitude in the wilderness, as described in Psalm 78 and Numbers 11, reflects a lack of gratitude for God's provision, despite the miraculous ways in which He had taken care of them. The manna, the bread from heaven, was an extraordinary provision, yet they grumbled because it did not meet their personal tastes. They longed for the familiarity of Egypt's food, forgetting the slavery they had suffered there. They were so focused on their own desires that they failed to recognize the greater blessing that God had given them.

The flowing water from the rock was another miraculous provision, but again, they doubted God's ability to provide beyond their expectations, asking for meat to eat, and questioning why God could not give them the luxuries they were used to in Egypt. Their grumbling revealed a deep-seated lack of faith, and a refusal to trust in God's sufficiency for their needs, even though He had already demonstrated His power.

The Parallel for Us Today

Like the Israelites, we too can be guilty of forgetting God's goodness in our lives. It's easy to take for granted the many blessings we receive daily, whether it's the provision of food, health, or the small moments of grace in our lives. Sometimes, when life doesn't meet our expectations or we face challenges, we too begin to complain and grumble, forgetting all that God has already done for us.

We might even ask for things that are outside of God's will or better plan for us, just as the Israelites demanded meat when God had already given them all they needed. We might wish for a "better" life or a more comfortable situation, overlooking the blessings we already have.

When people speak in repentance, but then their actions do not align with God's will, this is empty repentance—it is not genuine and reflects a heart that has not fully yielded to God's commands. True repentance involves a change of heart, a turning away from sin and a turning toward God's ways, trusting in His timing and provision.

Trials as a Test of Faith

Trials serve as a test of faith, both for Israel and for believers today. God allowed His people to experience hardships not because He was unkind, but because He was testing their hearts—to see if they would trust Him and remain faithful despite their circumstances. These trials were meant to build character, to strengthen their faith, and to help them rely more fully on God.

Just as Israel's faith was tested in the wilderness, so too are we tested in various ways throughout our lives. But these trials are not for nothing. As Peter says in 1 Peter 5:10, after we have "suffered a little while," God will perfect, strengthen, confirm, and establish us. It is through trials that we learn to cling more closely to God and grow in our trust in His ability to provide, sustain, and guide us through the wilderness of life.

Lessons on Gratitude, Obedience, and Faith

The key takeaway from Israel's story is that gratitude and obedience go hand-in-hand. Gratitude for

God's provision leads to a heart of obedience, and a life lived in obedience leads to greater blessing and faithfulness from God. However, when we are ungrateful, we fail to see God's provision in our lives, and we become discontent and prone to complaining.

Repentance is also significant. True repentance is not just saying the right words; it's about turning away from sin, trusting in God, and acting in alignment with His will. Israel's history shows us that even in times of disobedience, God's mercy is still available, but it is often through repentance and trust in His grace that we find restoration and growth.

In summary, the lessons from Israel's wilderness journey are deeply relevant for us today. We are called to trust in God's provision, be grateful for what He has given, and remain obedient to His commands, even when life doesn't go as we expect. Our trials are not in vain—they are opportunities for our faith to be refined and for us to become stronger in our dependence on God. And ultimately, as we turn to Him in repentance and faith, we can experience the fullness of His grace and His perfect plans for our lives.

And they remembered that God was their rock, and the high God their redeemer. Psalm 78:35 KJV

In times of trouble, human nature often leads people to cry out to God—especially when everything seems to be against us. It's during these moments of distress and uncertainty that the Rock—Jesus Christ, the living stone—becomes our refuge and strength. When we are in the wilderness of life, we often remember God as the Rock that sustains us, just as He sustained the Israelites in the desert.

Christ as the Living Rock

This reflection connects well with 1 Peter 2:4, where Peter writes about Jesus as the Living Stone, rejected by men but chosen by God. This rejection is central to the Gospel story—Jesus came to His own people, but they did not recognize Him, as you rightly mentioned. Even though He was the Messiah they had been waiting for, the chosen Rock of God's salvation, He was ultimately rejected, disallowed by men. This rejection culminated in His crucifixion, where He was "smitten" for our sins, just as the rock in the wilderness was struck to provide water for the Israelites.

However, the rejection of Christ by the world does not cancel His divine calling or purpose. As 1 Peter 2:6 affirms, Christ is the cornerstone, the foundation upon which our faith rests. This living stone is both rejected and chosen—rejected by men but chosen by God to be the source of life and salvation for those who believe.

Remembering the Rock in Affliction

You also draw attention to the way affliction often serves as a reminder of God's faithfulness. Deuteronomy 32:15 speaks of how the Israelites, in their prosperity, forgot God—their Rock, their provider, and protector. But in affliction, they remembered Him. It's in those moments of difficulty and distress that people often turn back to God, just as the Israelites remembered the Rock who had delivered them from Egypt.

God, being the Rock, is unchanging, faithful, and steadfast—even when we forget Him in times of ease. The same Rock that provided for Israel in the wilderness is the Rock that sustains us today, and Jesus Christ is the Rock that will never fail us.

Isaiah's Foretelling of Christ

As you mentioned, Isaiah also prophesied of the coming Messiah, pointing to Jesus as the Rock of our salvation. In Isaiah 28:16, the prophet writes, "So this is what the Sovereign Lord says: 'See, I lay a stone in Zion, a tested stone, a precious cornerstone for a sure foundation; the one who relies on it will never be stricken with panic.'" Here, Isaiah speaks of a stone that will be the foundation of God's work—Jesus Christ, who would be rejected by some but be the cornerstone for all who believe.

This cornerstone imagery connects directly to the Rock that is Christ. He is the foundation of everything we believe and the source of salvation. In times of crisis, we can stand firm because we know our faith is built upon the solid Rock that is Jesus Christ. When the storms of life come, we need not fear, for He is our Refuge and Strength (Psalm 46:1), and He will never leave nor forsake us (Hebrews 13:5).

The Affliction That Leads to Restoration

You also note that the affliction of God's people can be a means by which they remember Him. Just as the Israelites were reminded of God's goodness in their affliction, we too often find that in our trials and suffering, we are drawn closer to Christ. In Isaiah 53, the Suffering Servant is described Jesus The Christ, who would bear the pain and sin of the world, and yet through His suffering, He would bring healing and restoration.

It is often through these difficult times that God's people find a deeper dependence on Him. When all else fails, we remember that our faith is built upon the Rock of Christ, who is unshakable and eternal.

Key Takeaways

Christ as the Rock: Just as the rock in the wilderness provided water for Israel, Jesus Christ provides the living water of salvation for all who come to Him. He is our strength, refuge, and cornerstone.

Remembering God in Affliction: Sometimes, it takes difficulty and affliction to remind us of God's goodness and faithfulness. As the Israelites were reminded of their need for God in their distress, we too must turn to Christ, the living Rock, for our hope and salvation.

The Rejection and Choice of Christ: Though He was rejected by men, Christ is the chosen cornerstone of God's salvation. Our faith is built on this Rock, and no matter the trials or opposition we face, we can stand firm because Christ is unshakable.

In conclusion, your reflection beautifully ties together the idea of Christ being the Rock—the eternal, unchanging source of our salvation, provision, and protection. In times of trouble, we must remember to call out to the Rock, who is Jesus Christ, our Savior and strength.

Therefore, thus saith the Lord God, Behold, I lay in Zion for a foundation a stone, a tried stone, a precious corner stone, a sure foundation: he that believeth shall not make haste. Isaiah 28:16 KJV

Let's look at the foundational role of Jesus Christ in our faith and underscores the importance of making Him the centre of our lives. Jesus is the Rock, and building our faith on Him ensures that we will not be put to shame. 1 Peter 2:6-8 draws a sharp contrast between those who believe in Christ as the precious cornerstone and those who reject Him, ultimately becoming "a stone of stumbling and a rock of offense." The choice is clear: either we build on Christ, the firm foundation, or we stumble by rejecting Him.

Understanding Jesus: A Relationship through the Word

Your insight about the necessity of truly knowing

Jesus is critical. As you noted, understanding Jesus isn't merely about reading the Word of God, but about studying and meditating on it with the help of the Holy Spirit. This distinction is important because reading the Bible can sometimes be a passive act, while studying it—especially with the guidance of the Holy Spirit—helps to unlock its deeper truths. Jesus is revealed through the Scriptures, and only by growing in relationship with Him through the Word can we truly understand His nature and what He has done for us.

In John 14:26, Jesus promises the Holy Spirit as our Helper, who will teach us all things and bring to remembrance all that He has said. This is essential because, without the Holy Spirit's guidance, our understanding can be clouded by our own limited human perspective. Jesus is the Word (John 1:1) and it's only through spiritual illumination that we come to understand who He truly is—our Savior, Rock, and Cornerstone.

Jesus: The Rock of Refuge or the Stone of Stumbling?

As you rightly pointed out, Jesus can be one of two things depending on how we respond to Him: either a Rock of refuge for those who believe or a stone of stumbling for those who reject Him. In Isaiah 28:16, God promises to lay a stone in Zion, a precious cornerstone, and that those who believe in Him will not be put to shame. This is reiterated in 1 Peter 2:6, where Jesus is called the chosen and precious cornerstone.

However, for those who reject this stone, He becomes a stone of stumbling and a rock of offense, as they fall into judgment and destruction.

The decision is ours: Will we see Jesus as our Rock of salvation, a firm foundation upon which to build our lives, or will we reject Him and stumble? The challenge is clear. To believe in Jesus is to trust in Him as the foundation of our lives. But rejecting Him leads to spiritual ruin.

Building Your Life on a Firm Foundation
You emphasized the importance of building on a firm foundation, and this is one of the most significant aspects of the Christian life. Jesus, as the precious cornerstone, is the only foundation that can withstand the trials and storms of life. Matthew 7:24-27 gives the analogy of the wise man who builds his house on the rock versus the foolish man who builds on the sand. The wise man, who builds on Christ, will withstand the storms, while the foolish man will fall.

Job's Question: "Where then is my hope? Who can see any hope for me?" (Job 17:15) is a poignant reminder of the uncertainty of life without a firm foundation. Job, in the midst of his trials, asks the question that many of us must ask in times of suffering: where is our hope? Our hope is in the Rock, Jesus Christ, the foundation of our faith. He is the one who gives us strength in the face of adversity, providing living water in our spiritual thirst and giving us an eternal refuge.

Key Takeaways

Jesus is the Rock and Foundation of Our Faith: Building our lives on Jesus Christ, the precious cornerstone, ensures that we are rooted in eternal security and will not be put to shame.

The Need for True Understanding of Jesus: To know Jesus is not just to read about Him, but to study the Word with the help of the Holy Spirit. This understanding transforms us and brings us into a deeper relationship with Him.

Jesus: The Rock of Refuge or the Stone of Stumbling: Jesus is either a Rock of refuge for those who believe in Him or a stone of stumbling for those who reject Him. The decision to trust or reject Christ has eternal consequences.

Building on a Firm Foundation: Life without Christ is like building a house on sand—unstable and doomed to collapse. Jesus is the solid foundation on which we must build our faith, for only He can withstand the storms of life.

In conclusion, your reflection calls us to examine our response to Jesus Christ, the Rock. He is the firm foundation that provides hope, strength, and security in a world full of instability. When we build our lives on Him, we find refuge, eternal life, and a foundation that will never fail.

But where shall wisdom be found? and where is the place of understanding? Man knoweth not the price thereof; neither is it found in the land of the living. Job 28:12-13 KJV

The Limitations of Human Wisdom
When we rely on human wisdom, we often miss the deeper, eternal truths that God has revealed in His Word. Proverbs 3:5-6 urges us to "Trust in the Lord with all your heart and lean not on your own understanding." This reminder highlights the natural tendency to seek answers and solutions from our own knowledge or the world's wisdom, yet it's clear that God's wisdom is far superior. As you mentioned, it's easy to forget the importance of God's Word when we are so preoccupied with seeking answers through our own means.

The world offers temporary solutions, yet God's wisdom is eternal, rooted in His truth, love, and purpose for our lives. As Isaiah 55:8-9 reminds us, God's ways are higher than our ways, and His thoughts are higher than our thoughts. When we align ourselves with His wisdom through His Word, we gain the insight needed to navigate life's challenges, not based on what the world offers but on what God reveals.

Seeking God's Wisdom in the Bible
God's wisdom is revealed in the Bible, and it's only through the study of Scripture that we can understand the deeper things of God. As you rightly

point out, we must look beyond the confines of human understanding and seek God's wisdom through the guidance of His Word. The Bible is not just a collection of ancient stories but a living and active guide for life. 2 Timothy 3:16-17 affirms that all Scripture is inspired by God and is useful for teaching, rebuking, correcting, and training in righteousness. Through God's Word, we discover the wisdom that can only be found in Him.

Jesus: Our Spiritual Rock
As you pointed out, Jesus is the Spiritual Rock that we must trust as our refuge and deliverer. He is the Rock of Ages and the only foundation upon which we can build our lives. 2 Samuel 22:2-3 beautifully portrays God as the fortress, deliverer, shield, and horn of salvation—He is our high tower, refuge, and Savior. These attributes remind us of the strength and security we find in God alone.

When we face trials, we are called to trust in Christ as the Rock of our salvation. Jesus is the only firm foundation that can withstand the storms of life. Psalm 18:2 echoes this truth, stating, "The Lord is my rock, my fortress, and my deliverer; my God is my rock, in whom I take refuge." This reminder is vital: no earthly thing, no matter how valuable or comforting, can provide the same security and hope as Jesus, our Rock.

Trusting God Alone as Our Refuge
In moments of doubt, struggle, or uncertainty, it's easy to forget that God is our refuge and strength

(Psalm 46:1). The world offers many temporary solutions —wealth, success, or human wisdom—but only God can provide the true refuge and deliverance we need. He is our high tower, our place of safety, and He alone is worthy of our trust.

As Proverbs 2:6 reminds us, "For the Lord gives wisdom; from His mouth come knowledge and understanding." It is in trusting Him fully, not in our own understanding, that we find peace and stability. Jesus, as the Spiritual Rock, offers us living water and the wisdom needed for eternal life.

Believe me that I am in the Father, and the Father in me: or else believe me for the very works' sake. John 14:11

1. Christ as the Exclusive Way to the Father (John 14:6)

Jesus' statement in John 14:6 is one of the most exclusive and definitive statements in Christian theology: "I am the way, the truth, and the life. No one comes to the Father except through me." This is not just a declaration of Jesus' role as a teacher or prophet but an assertion of His divine identity. In this passage, Jesus is emphasizing that the path to God cannot be found in any other person, ideology, or religion.

The Way: Jesus is the only way to salvation. There are no other paths or intermediaries. His life, death, and resurrection are the only means by which sinful humanity can be reconciled to a holy God.

The Truth: Jesus embodies truth itself, as He is the fulfilment of God's promises and revelation to humanity. The truth He speaks is not just moral wisdom or ethical guidance, but the ultimate reality about God, sin, salvation, and eternal life.

The Life: Jesus offers eternal life, not only after death but in the here and now. His life is a living example of God's righteousness, and His sacrifice makes eternal life possible for those who believe in Him.

This declaration aligns with Christ's divinity, as He asserts that only through Him can humanity access the Father. John 10:30 reinforces this: "I and the Father are one." The perfect unity between Jesus and the Father establishes the foundation of the Christian doctrine of the Trinity, where the Father, Son, and Holy Spirit are distinct but share in the same divine essence.

2. Christ as Our Mediator and Advocate (1 Timothy 2:5; 1 John 2:1)

As the Mediator, Jesus stands between God and humanity, bridging the chasm that sin has created. 1 Timothy 2:5 emphasizes His unique role: "For there is one God and one mediator between God and mankind, the man Christ Jesus." Jesus, in His humanity, represents us before the Father, and in His divinity, He can offer a sacrifice sufficient to reconcile us to God. His atoning sacrifice on the cross is the basis of this mediation.

As our Advocate (1 John 2:1), Jesus not only mediates between us and the Father but also defends us before God. When we sin, He is our righteous advocate, interceding on our behalf. He pleads our case, not based on our own merit but on the basis of His righteousness and finished work on the cross. This assures believers that, even though they fail, they are not condemned because of Christ's eternal and effective advocacy.

3. Christ as the Spiritual Rock and Foundation of Our Faith

Christ as the Spiritual Rock draws from 1 Corinthians 10:4, where Paul describes Christ as the Rock that sustained the Israelites in the wilderness: "and the rock was Christ." Just as the Israelites depended on the rock for water, believers depend on Christ for spiritual nourishment and sustenance. Jesus is the source of living water (John 4:10, 7:37), offering the Holy Spirit to all who believe in Him.

In Matthew 7:24-25, Jesus likens His words to a rock-solid foundation for life. A believer's life, built on Christ's teachings and redemptive work, will withstand the trials and challenges of life, much like a house built on a rock will withstand storms. Jesus Himself is the foundation of the Church (Matthew 16:18), and the cornerstone of our faith (Ephesians 2:20).

4. The Unity of Christ and the Father
the unity between Jesus and the Father is central

to understanding both His divinity and His role in salvation. Jesus is not a mere representative of God but is in perfect unity with the Father. In John 10:30, He states, "I and the Father are one." This unity goes beyond function (what they do) to essence (who they are). Jesus' divinity means that He shares in the fullness of God's nature, and His works are a revelation of God Himself.

This truth is foundational for understanding the Trinity. Jesus, the Son, is one with the Father and the Holy Spirit, and their works are united in purpose and action. Jesus, as the perfect revelation of God's holiness, is not only fully divine but also fully human, making Him the perfect Savior and mediator for all humanity.

Behold, I will stand before thee there upon the rock in Horeb; and thou shalt smite the rock, and there shall come water out of it, that the people may drink. And Moses did so in the sight of the elders of Israel. Exodus 17:6 KJV

The doctrine of Christ's divinity, His role as the Way to the Father, and His perfect life as a revelation of God's holiness are central themes in Christian theology. These truths illuminate the unique position of Jesus Christ as the ultimate revelation of God, the exclusive means of salvation, and the foundation of Christian faith.

1. Christ's Divinity

Jesus Christ is fully divine and fully human, a mystery at the heart of Christian belief. His divinity is essential for understanding His role in salvation. If Jesus were not God, His death on the cross could not have been sufficient to atone for the sins of humanity. His divine nature guarantees the infinite worth of His sacrifice. The doctrine of the Trinity teaches that Jesus is the Son of God, one with the Father and the Holy Spirit, co-equal and co-eternal in the Godhead.

John 1:1-14 declares that Jesus is the Word made flesh, and through Him, all things were created. His divinity is evident throughout the Gospels, as He performs miracles, forgives sins, and speaks with divine authority.

John 10:30: "I and the Father are one," emphasizes His unity with the Father. This unity is not just in purpose but in essence and nature.

2. Jesus as the Way to the Father

In John 14:6, Jesus says, "I am the way, the truth, and the life. No one comes to the Father except through me." This statement is profound, as it asserts that Jesus is the exclusive means by which humanity can be reconciled to God. There is no other path to salvation. He is not merely a teacher or prophet; He is the mediator between God and man (1 Timothy 2:5).

Acts 4:12 further reinforces this exclusivity: "There is no other name under heaven given among men by which we must be saved." Jesus is the only way to the Father because, as both God and man, He alone could bridge the gap caused by sin.

His atoning sacrifice on the cross is the means by

which humanity can be restored to a right relationship with God. Through His death, Jesus opens the way for forgiveness, reconciliation, and eternal life with God.

3. Christ's Perfect Life as a Revelation of God's Holiness

Jesus is the perfect revelation of God's holiness. His life, free from sin, shows us who God is in both His character and nature. Jesus revealed the Father's heart through His teachings, His actions, and His compassion. Through Him, we see the fullness of God's grace, mercy, justice, and truth.

Hebrews 1:3 describes Jesus as "the radiance of the glory of God and the exact imprint of His nature," meaning that Jesus perfectly reflects the holiness and purity of God.

1 John 3:5 reminds us that "in Him there is no sin." His perfect obedience to the Father's will serves as the model for believers.

Jesus' sinlessness not only reveals God's holiness but also makes Him the perfect sacrifice for sin. He lived a life of complete obedience, something that all of humanity failed to do. This is why His death on the cross was necessary: He took our place and paid the price for sin, though He Himself was without sin.

4. Jesus as the Spiritual Rock and Foundation of Faith

The metaphor of Jesus as the Spiritual Rock comes from 1 Corinthians 10:4, where Paul writes, "and the rock was Christ." Just as the rock in the wilderness (which Moses struck to provide water) sustained the Israelites physically, Christ as the Spiritual Rock sustains believers spiritually. From Him flows the living water of the Holy Spirit, the source of eternal life for all who believe in Him (John 4:10, 7:37).

In Matthew 7:24-25, Jesus teaches that those who hear His words and put them into practice are like a man who builds his house on the rock—a firm foundation that can withstand any storm. Jesus Himself is the rock-solid foundation upon which the Christian life is built. His life, death, and resurrection form the bedrock of the faith.

Jesus as the foundation (Matthew 16:18) and cornerstone (Ephesians 2:20) of the Church signifies that all believers are united in Him. The Church is built on Christ, the living stone (1 Peter 2:4), and He is the unshakable foundation for every believer's life.

5. Testifying to the Unity of Christ and the Father

The unity between the Father and the Son is not just functional, but ontological—it is rooted in their very essence. Jesus is not an agent of God, but He shares the same divine nature as the Father. The works that Jesus performed—miracles, healings, forgiveness of sins—are manifestations of the Father's will.

In John 14:9, Jesus tells Philip, "Whoever has

seen me has seen the Father." This profound statement underscores that Christ reveals the Father's nature perfectly.

As the Son, Jesus is always in perfect harmony with the Father. Their unity reflects the perfect communion within the Godhead, further emphasizing the importance of relationship in Christian faith.

Conclusion

In summary, the doctrine of Christ's divinity teaches that He is fully God and fully man, and through His divine nature, He makes salvation possible. His role as the Way to the Father is unique and exclusive, and His perfect life reveals the holiness and righteousness of God. As the Spiritual Rock, He is the foundation of our faith, offering life and sustenance to all who believe in Him.

Ultimately, Jesus Christ's works testify to His unity with the Father, and through Him, believers are brought into relationship with God. His sacrifice on the cross, His intercession as our Advocate, and His role as the foundation of our faith are at the heart of the Christian gospel. In Him alone, we find salvation, life, and hope—the very essence of God's grace and truth.

CHAPTER THREE
JESUS THE SACRIFICE

Christ The Promise Lamb

And I will put enmity between you and the woman, and between your seed and her Seed; He shall bruise your head, and you shall bruise His heel (Genesis 3:15).

Let's examine what Genesis 3:15 is communicating, as this verse has been interpreted in various ways. From our study, several conclusions can be drawn:

The "seed of the woman" refers to the promised Messiah—specifically, the one who would redeem humanity, tracing back to Adam, who surrendered the authority God originally gave him over all creation (Genesis 1:28) to Satan. Satan, by planting seeds of doubt, led humanity into disobedience against God, causing people to become, as 1 John 3:10 describes, "children of the devil." The ultimate fulfilment of this promise is found in Christ.

The "bruised heel" of the woman's seed symbolizes the crucifixion of Christ. Through a woman, God brought the Messiah into the world, one who would suffer death but rise again, reclaiming what humanity had lost in Eden. Because of Jesus' resurrection, He now holds the keys of death and hell (Revelation 1:18), restoring humanity's hope and authority.

The "bruised head" of the serpent points to the ultimate judgment of Satan (Revelation 20:10), signifying his final defeat and the end of his influence over humanity.

Turning to the Old Testament, we find numerous prophecies about the coming of Christ as a "guilt offering." Jesus is depicted as the perfect, divinely provided sacrifice, the only one able to fully atone for the sins of God's people. Through His life, death, and resurrection, Jesus fulfilled the complete payment required for sin, offering redemption to all who believe in Him.

Yet it pleased the Lord to bruise him; he hath put him to grief: when thou shalt make his soul an offering for sin, he shall see his seed, he shall prolong his days, and the pleasure of the Lord shall prosper in his hand. Isaiah 53:10 KJV

Absolutely! The unique nature of Jesus Christ as both fully God and fully man, made Him the only one capable of bridging the chasm between a holy God and sinful humanity. Since all humans inherit sin from Adam (Romans 5:12), no ordinary person could fulfil the requirements of a perfect sacrifice. Sin demanded a substitute who was not only sinless but also capable of bearing the weight of humanity's transgressions.

Jesus, being God incarnate (John 1:14), lived a life free from sin (2 Corinthians 5:21), qualifying Him as the perfect Lamb of God who takes away the sin of the world (John 1:29). His divine nature ensured His ability to meet the demands of God's holiness, while His human nature allowed Him to represent humanity fully. This dual nature is what made His sacrifice on the cross effective and sufficient.

Through His death and resurrection, Jesus not only atoned for sin but also reconciled us to God, creating a way for humanity to be restored to fellowship with Him (Romans 5:10). His work on the cross is the ultimate demonstration of God's love and justice, where mercy triumphs over judgment for all who believe (James 2:13, John 3:16).

Indeed, the first Passover in Egypt serves as a profound and prophetic foreshadowing of Christ's redemptive work. The instructions given in Exodus 12:11-13 to apply the lamb's blood to the doorposts symbolized a divine covering that spared the Israelites from the judgment of death. This act pointed forward to the ultimate sacrifice of Jesus, whose blood provides eternal deliverance from sin and death for all who believe.

Paul's declaration in 1 Corinthians 5:7, "For Christ, our Passover lamb, has been sacrificed," connects the dots between the Old Testament ritual and the New Testament reality. Just as the lamb's blood was a sign of protection during the first Passover, Jesus' blood now marks believers, shielding them from the eternal consequences of sin and granting them access to eternal life.

The timing of Jesus' death at the evening sacrifice further underscores His role as the fulfilment of the Old Testament sacrificial system. The temple sacrifices, instituted to atone for sin, pointed forward to a greater sacrifice—one that would fully and finally satisfy God's justice. Hebrews 9:12 highlights this fulfilment, stating that Jesus entered the Most Holy Place "once for all by his own blood, thus obtaining eternal redemption."

Christ's death also aligns with the broader themes of deliverance and freedom. Just as the first Passover marked the Israelites' liberation from slavery in Egypt, Jesus' sacrifice liberates humanity from the bondage of sin and death (Romans 6:22). His work on the cross is the culmination of God's plan to redeem and restore, fulfilling every Old Testament shadow with the reality of His grace.

This connection between the Passover lamb and

Christ's sacrifice reveals the unity of Scripture and the depth of God's redemptive plan. It invites believers to see Jesus not only as their Savior but also as the central figure in God's unfolding story of salvation—a story that began in Eden, was foretold in Egypt, and was fulfilled on Calvary.

The prophets, including Isaiah and Jeremiah, provided glimpses of this redemptive plan centuries before its fulfilment. Isaiah 53:7 poignantly describes the suffering servant as "like a lamb led to the slaughter," bearing our iniquities and providing healing through His wounds. Jeremiah similarly portrays the suffering servant as one who would be rejected and slain for others. These prophecies, though often misunderstood in their time, find their ultimate meaning in Jesus, whose life and death perfectly fulfilled their descriptions.

The early church fathers, reflecting on these Scriptures, recognized the seamless connection between the Old and New Testaments. They saw in Jesus the true "bread of life" (John 6:35), the sacrificial lamb who nourishes and sustains all who come to Him in faith. His death not only fulfilled the letter of the prophecies but also their profound spiritual implications: that through His sacrifice, humanity could be reconciled to God.

This grand narrative of salvation reveals God's meticulous and loving plan, spanning generations and culminating in the cross. It's a call to believers to see the continuity of Scripture, the sovereignty of God, and the depth of His love. As the true Passover Lamb, Jesus' sacrifice is both the climax of redemptive history and the foundation of eternal life for all who believe in Him.

In texts like Isaiah 53, the suffering and rejection of the Servant are portrayed vividly: He would be "cut off from the land of the living" (Isaiah 53:8), with His suffering serving a redemptive purpose. These passages became central to the early Church's understanding of Christ's sacrifice, viewing them as profound examples of how the Scriptures prepared the way for Christ's redemptive work.

Indeed, as Romans 3:23 reminds us, "all have sinned and fall short of the glory of God," but the story doesn't end there. Through Jesus, we find hope, redemption, and restoration. His sacrifice on the cross, foretold in Isaiah 53:5 — "But He was pierced for our transgressions, He was crushed for our iniquities; the punishment that brought us peace was on Him, and by His wounds, we are healed" — is the ultimate expression of God's boundless love and mercy.

In His suffering, Jesus bore the full weight of our sin, taking the punishment, we deserved, so that we might be reconciled with God. And because of His resurrection, we are given new life, free from the chains of sin and death. This gift, freely given, calls us to live in gratitude, striving to walk in His ways and share His love with others.

The call to "take up our cross" is a profound reminder of the cost of discipleship. Jesus' words in Luke 14:27 challenge us to embrace the sacrifices, trials, and challenges that come with living as His followers. Just as Christ bore His cross out of love and obedience to the Father, we are invited to bear ours as an expression of our devotion to Him.

Our personal crosses may take many forms—persevering through trials, resisting temptations, standing firm in faith amidst opposition, or surrendering our own desires for the sake of God's will. These experiences refine us and draw us closer to Christ, shaping us into His likeness. As Paul writes in Romans 8:17, "If we are children, then we are heirs—heirs of God and co-heirs with Christ, if indeed we share in His sufferings in order that we may also share in His glory."

Bearing our cross is not about enduring hardship for its own sake but about surrendering ourselves fully to God's purpose. It is through this surrender that we find true life, as Jesus assures us: "Whoever wants to save their life will lose it, but whoever loses their life for me will find it" (Matthew 16:25).

In every trial, we are reminded that we do not bear our burdens alone. Christ walks with us, giving us the strength to endure and the grace to remain faithful. May we daily take up our cross with joy and steadfastness, trusting in His promise of eternal life.

The path to salvation indeed runs through the cross of Christ, who bore the weight of our sins and conquered death on our behalf. As Paul writes in Romans 4:25, "He was delivered over to death for our sins and was raised to life for our justification." Jesus' suffering was not in vain; it accomplished the ultimate purpose of reconciling us to God and opening the way for eternal life.

Through His sacrifice, we have been gifted the Holy Spirit, who dwells within us, sanctifying and empowering us to live in obedience and love. It is by His grace alone that we are cleansed and made new, for as Isaiah 1:18 declares, "Though your sins are like scarlet, they shall be as white as snow."

Because of Christ's unimaginable suffering, we can endure our own trials with hope and joy, knowing that they pale in comparison to the eternal glory awaiting us. As Paul encourages in Philippians 3:8, "I consider everything a loss because of the surpassing worth of knowing Christ Jesus my Lord, for whose sake I have lost all things." This perspective reminds us to place our love, trust, and devotion entirely in Him, who loved us first and gave Himself for us.

Jesus Christ, the Lamb of God, is truly our Redeemer and Savior. His sacrifice on the cross has secured our redemption and granted us the promise of eternal fellowship with God. May we live every day in grateful response, loving and serving Him with all our hearts.

When the even was come, they brought unto him many that were possessed with devils: and he cast out the spirits with his word and healed all that were sick:17 That it might be fulfilled which was spoken by Isaiah the prophet, saying, Himself took our infirmities, and bare our sicknesses. Matthew 8: 16-17

Jesus' redemptive work indeed extends to both our spiritual and physical needs, revealing the fullness of His compassion and the depth of His love for humanity. As foretold in Isaiah 53:4-5, "Surely He took up our pain and bore our suffering... He was pierced for our transgressions, He was crushed for our iniquities; the punishment that brought us peace was on Him, and by His wounds, we are healed."

This passage highlights how Jesus bore not only the weight of our sins but also our afflictions, offering healing and restoration through His atonement. His ministry on earth was a testament to this truth—He healed the sick, cast out demons, and forgave sins, demonstrating that His mission was holistic, addressing both body and soul.

John the Baptist's declaration in John 1:29, "Behold, the Lamb of God, who takes away the sin of the world!" underscores Jesus' role as the ultimate sacrificial Lamb, whose death would remove the barrier of sin separating us from God. In His bruising and crushing, He defeated the power of sin and death, restoring us to a right relationship with our Creator.

Through His sacrifice, Jesus reconciled us to God, fulfilling the words of 2 Corinthians 5:18-19: "All this is from God, who reconciled us to Himself through Christ and gave us the ministry of reconciliation: that God was reconciling the world to Himself in Christ, not counting people's sins against them." This reconciliation not only grants us spiritual freedom but also empowers us to live as new creations, reflecting His love and grace in every area of our lives.

Indeed, no prophet or mere man could bear the full weight of humanity's sins and infirmities—this profound act required someone who is both fully divine and fully human. Jesus, the spotless Lamb of God, was uniquely qualified for this mission because of His sinless nature and divine authority.

Through His sacrifice, He demonstrated perfect love and perfect obedience to the Father, accomplishing what no one else could. As Hebrews 7:26-27 states, "Such a high priest truly meets our need—one who is holy, blameless, pure, set apart from sinners, exalted above the heavens. Unlike the other high priests, He does not need to offer sacrifices day after day... He sacrificed for their sins once for all when He offered Himself."

It is this truth that sets Christianity apart: salvation is not something we can achieve through human effort or merit. It is the gift of grace made possible only by the finished work of Christ, the Son of God, who willingly gave His life for us. His divinity ensures the infinite value of His sacrifice, and His humanity allows Him to fully identify with our weaknesses and sufferings (Hebrews 4:15).

The next day John seeth Jesus coming unto him, and saith, Behold the Lamb of God, which taketh away the sin of the world. John 1: 29 KJV

In the Old Testament, the lamb was central to sacrifices, particularly during the Passover (Exodus 12) and as a sin offering (Leviticus 4:32-35). The lamb served as a symbol for removing sin, guilt, and the punishment we deserved, as people laid their sins upon it—foreshadowing Christ, whom John the Baptist proclaimed as the "Lamb of God who takes away the sins of the world." Isaiah 53:10 reveals that it pleased God to allow the suffering of His Servant. As explained in the Dake's Bible, this was because the sacrifice was the only way to redeem humanity, fulfilling God's redemptive plan. Through Christ's ultimate sacrifice, the guilt and penalty of sin are lifted from those who believe.

The only reason it pleased Jehovah to permit Him to be crucified was to bring about the redemption of the whole creation so that His eternal program could be carried out with man on earth. He could not have been pleased with the mutilation of his beloved Son because He punished men for this (Acts 2:22-24; 1 Thessalonians 2:15-16). Both the Father and the Son volunteered to suffer such indignities for the salvation of men (John 3:16; 10:18). Such a sacrifice on the part of God showed His divine perfection, justice, mercy, and boundless benevolence. The law was upheld, sin was judged, and a basis of pardon and eternal reconciliation was made possible.

The book of Hebrews exalts Christ as supreme, even above the angels. The name given to the Son, Jesus, is so powerful that "every knee shall bow" (Philippians 2:10). Hebrews also reveals that God, through His Son, created the world (Hebrews 1:2; John 1:3; Colossians 1:16). At the appointed time, God revealed Himself fully through Jesus, allowing us to understand His perfect will. Jesus' obedience to the Father, even to the point of death, provides the ultimate example of faithful devotion. Jesus is the complete expression of God in human form; as He said, "Anyone who has seen me has seen the Father" (John 14:9; Hebrews 1:1-4).

The sacrifice of Jesus indeed fulfilled what the old covenant could not accomplish. The book of Hebrews provides a powerful explanation of this truth, showing how Christ is the fulfilment of God's plan for redemption. As Hebrews 8:7-10 explains, the old covenant, based on the Law, was limited in its ability to bring complete and lasting forgiveness for sin. It served as a shadow of the better things to come (Hebrews 10:1), pointing forward to the perfect sacrifice that only Jesus could offer.

Under the old covenant, repeated sacrifices were required, but they could not fully cleanse the conscience or remove sin permanently (Hebrews 10:4). However, through His death and resurrection, Christ established a new covenant, one written not on tablets of stone but on the hearts of His people, as foretold in Jeremiah 31:33 and reiterated in Hebrews 8:10: "This is the covenant I will establish with the people of Israel after that time, declares the Lord. I will put my laws in their minds and write them on their hearts. I will be their God, and they will be my people."

Jesus became the ultimate and final sacrifice, offering His body once for all to take away sin (Hebrews 9:26-28). Through His blood, we are cleansed, sanctified, and brought into a new relationship with God. This new covenant provides what the old could not: complete redemption, reconciliation, and eternal access to God through faith in Christ.

This fulfilment of God's promise reminds us of His faithfulness and love. It calls us to respond with gratitude, obedience, and trust in the finished work of Christ, who is now seated at the right hand of the Father, interceding for us as our perfect High Priest. What a beautiful, life-giving truth! Hallelujah for the new covenant established through Jesus Christ!

For if that first covenant had been faultless, then should no place have been sought for the second. For finding fault with them, he saith, Behold, the days come, saith the Lord, when I will make a new covenant with the house of Israel and with the house of Judah: Not according to the covenant that I made with their fathers in the day when I took them by the hand to lead them out of the land of Egypt; because they continued not in my covenant, and I regarded them not, saith the Lord. For this is the covenant that I will make with the house of Israel after those days, saith the Lord; I will put my laws into their mind, and write them in their hearts: and I will be to them a God, and they shall be to me a people: Hebrews 8:7-10

Roy Hession, a Christian evangelist and author, is best known for his impactful book The Calvary Road, which beautifully emphasizes themes of repentance, humility, and revival in the Christian life. Hession writes profoundly about the Lamb of God and the incredible love Jesus demonstrated through His sacrifice. He highlights that it is only by understanding the depth of Christ's love and the cost of His atonement that we can fully grasp the grace offered to us.

Hession's reflections often focus on the humility of Jesus, the selflessness of His sacrifice, and the call for believers to walk in that same humility and brokenness. His writings remind us that Jesus, as the Lamb of God, willingly took our place, bearing the penalty of sin out of

His great love for us—a love that seeks not just to redeem but also to transform us into His likeness.

He was also the spotless Lamb. Not only did nothing escape His lips, but there was nothing in His heart but love for those who had sent Him to the cross. There was no resentment towards them, no grudges, no bitterness. Even as they were putting the nails through his hands, He was murmuring, 'I love you,' and He asked His Father to forgive them too. He was willing to suffer it in meekness for us. But what resentment and bitterness have not we had in our hearts – toward this one and one, and over so much less than what they did to Jesus. Each reaction left a stain on our hearts, and the dove had to fly away because we were not willing to bear it and forgive it for Jesus' sake.

The differences between the Old and New Testaments are indeed profound, yet they also harmonize beautifully to reveal God's unfolding plan of redemption. The Old Testament lays the foundation, revealing God's character, His covenant with Israel, and His promises, while the New Testament fulfils those promises through Jesus Christ.

Here are a few examples, explain by the Dake's Annotated reference bible. Page 351.

Old Covenant
New Covenant
Came by Moses John 1:17   C a m e

by Christ Hebrew 8: 6; 9: 15	
Law of sin Rom. 7:23; 8:2	Law of Righteousness Rom. 9:31
Ended by Christ Rom.10:4	Started by Christ Heb. 8:6; 10:9
Brought death 2 Cor. 3:7	Brought life Rom. 8:2
A shadow Col. 2:14-17	The reality Heb. 10; 1-18
Fulfilled Mt. 5: 17-18	Now in force Heb. 8:6; 10; 9
Powerless to save Heb. 9:9; 10:4	save to uttermost Jn. 1:17; 3:16
Remembers Sins Heb. 10:3	Forgets Sin Heb. 8:12; 10:17
Ratified by animal blood Hebrew. 9: 16-22, Mt. 26:28	Ratified by the blood of Christ
Could not redeem 10; 4	Redeems Gal. 3:13 Heb. 9:12-15
Abolishment predicted Hos. 2:11	Establishment predicted Heb. 8:7
Made to change Gal.3; Heb. 9	Made Eternal Heb. 13:20
Cannot justify Gal. 2; 16	Can justify Acts 13: 38-39
Bring a curse Gal. 3: 10	Redeems from it Gal. 3:13
Exposes sin Gal. 3: 19	Covers sin Rom. 4;18
Under law Rom. 6: 14-15	Under grace Gal. 3:22-25

Abolished 2 Cor. 3;13   Remains 2 Cor. 3:11
Taken away Heb. 10:9   Not taken away 10:9
For Israel only, Dt. 4:7-8; 5: 3   For all men Mt. 26:28

Hebrews 9:14 tells us that only the blood of Jesus could cleanse us from our sins. Unlike the sacrifices of bulls or goats, Jesus offered Himself as the perfect sacrifice. The offering of oneself is the highest form of sacrifice, and in this case, it was the highest offering the universe could provide. Jesus, the Lamb of God, was "without spot" — meaning He was without any fault or defect, just as the sacrificial animals in the Old Testament had to be without blemish (Leviticus 1:10; Leviticus 22:17-22). He was neither lame, blind, nor diseased. Jesus, the perfect sacrifice, was without sin, pure and spotless, fulfilling the ultimate requirement for atonement.

The bible tells us this,

For such an high priest became us, who is holy, harmless, undefiled, separate from sinners, and made higher than the heavens; Hebrews 7: 26 KJV.

Christ's holiness, perfection, and divinity uniquely qualified Him to be our High Priest and the spotless Lamb of God. As the writer of Hebrews so powerfully explains, Jesus entered the holy place not by the blood of animals, as was the custom under the old covenant, but by His own blood, securing eternal redemption for us (Hebrews 9:12).

His sinless nature was essential for this role. Unlike every other human born into the world, Christ was conceived by the Holy Spirit, free from the sinful nature passed down through Adam (Luke 1:35). This made Him the only one capable of standing before God on our behalf. As 2 Corinthians 5:21 declares, "God made Him who had no sin to be sin for us, so that in Him we might become the righteousness of God."

As our High Priest, Jesus not only offers the perfect sacrifice—He is the perfect sacrifice. His offering of Himself was once for all, complete and sufficient for the forgiveness of sins (Hebrews 10:10). Through His work, He sanctifies us, bringing us into a holy relationship with God. By His righteousness, we are made clean, and by His blood, we are justified.

This truth calls us to worship and gratitude, for it is through Christ alone that we are reconciled to God. His divine nature and perfect obedience demonstrate the depth of God's love for us and the incredible lengths He went to in order to redeem us. Praise be to our holy Savior, the Lamb of God, who takes away the sins of the world!

In the Old Testament, the high priest was to excel in knowledge, beauty, and wealth, but the characteristic of our High Priest, Jesus, is purity and holiness (1 Peter 1:3-4). He surpasses even the angels in the holiness of His nature, setting Him apart from earthly priests who were burdened by infirmities. Jesus is the perfect, sinless sacrifice.

Knowing about Jesus—His life, miracles, and even His death—is not enough to save us. Salvation is not about intellectual understanding but about a personal relationship with Christ, grounded in faith and repentance. The cross is the turning point of history and the anchor of our salvation. It is where the price for our sins was paid in full, and only by embracing its power can we be transformed.

As Paul writes in Romans 10:9-10, "If you declare with your mouth, 'Jesus is Lord,' and believe in your heart that God raised Him from the dead, you will be saved. For it is with your heart that you believe and are justified, and it is with your mouth that you profess your faith and are saved." This belief is not merely intellectual assent but a deep, transformative faith that acknowledges Christ as both Savior and Lord.

The cleansing power of His blood is central to this transformation. Revelation 1:5 reminds us that Jesus "loves us and has freed us from our sins by His blood." Through the blood, He shed on the cross, we are purified, justified, and reconciled to God. But this cleansing requires repentance—a turning away from sin and toward God—and a wholehearted acceptance of Christ's lordship in our lives.

Without this personal encounter with the cross, we remain in our sins. As Jesus Himself said in John 8:24, "If you do not believe that I am He, you will indeed die in your sins." To know Christ is to experience the life-giving power of His sacrifice, to walk in the freedom and grace He provides, and to live in the assurance of eternal life.

CHAPTER FOUR
JESUS THE RISEN LORD

He is not here but is risen: remember how he spake unto you when he was yet in Galilee, Saying, The Son of man must be delivered into the hands of sinful men, and be crucified, and the third day rise again. Luke 24:6-8 KJV

The resurrection is indeed the central event of the Christian faith, for it signifies that the Son of God, Jesus Christ, died on the cross to pay the penalty for humanity's sins, offering everlasting life to all who believe. As John 3:16 declares, "For God so loved the world that He gave His one and only Son, that whoever believes in Him shall not perish but have eternal life."

On the day of the resurrection, everything changed. Death was conquered, and the penalty for sin was paid in full. Through Jesus' victory over death, mankind was given the hope of eternal life. Jesus, by His death and resurrection, opened the way for humanity to be reconciled with God. His sacrifice on the cross allows all who receive Him as Lord and Savior to be forgiven, redeemed, and raised to new life.

The resurrection assures us that death is not the

end; it is the beginning of eternal life with Christ. Through His blood, shed for us, Jesus made it possible for us to be reunited with God, not only in this life but forever. This is the hope that gives believers confidence in the face of death, knowing that through Jesus, we too will be raised to live with Him for all eternity.

Through the resurrection, the church is given the authority and power to proclaim the victory of Jesus Christ over death and sin, just as the apostles did. The resurrection is not just a historical event but a divine declaration that God's power is at work in the world and in the lives of believers.

As the apostle Paul writes in Ephesians 1:19-20, "I pray that the eyes of your heart may be enlightened in order that you may know the hope to which he has called you, the riches of his glorious inheritance in his holy people, and his incomparably great power for us who believe. That power is the same as the mighty strength he exerted when he raised Christ from the dead."

This resurrection power is available to the church today. It is a power that enables believers to endure trials and tragedies, knowing that even in the darkest moments, God's resurrection power can bring hope, healing, and new life.

Just as the apostles boldly proclaimed Christ as the risen Lord, we too are called to share this hope with the world. The resurrection assures us that no matter what comes our way, God's power is sufficient to sustain us and to give us victory over every challenge. It is through this power that we can confidently proclaim that Jesus is alive, and that through Him, there is hope for the future—both in this life and for all eternity.

Joseph Scheumann's point about the term "Easter" is an important one in the context of Christian theology and biblical terminology. The term "Easter" is not derived from the original biblical languages and is not the term used to describe the resurrection of Jesus in the Scriptures. Instead, the correct term should be "Resurrection Day", or as you mentioned, "Pascha" in Aramaic, which is the equivalent of the Hebrew "Pesach" (Passover).

The term "Pesach" in Hebrew refers to the Jewish festival of Passover, which commemorates God's deliverance of the Israelites from slavery in Egypt. In the Christian context, the resurrection of Jesus took place during the time of the Passover festival, and thus, "Pascha" became the term used by early Christians to refer to the celebration of Jesus' resurrection. This term underscores the continuity between Jesus as the "Lamb of God" who takes away the sins of the world (John 1:29) and the Jewish Passover lamb, whose blood marked the homes of the Israelites for deliverance.

The use of the term "Easter" in many parts of the world today is believed to have been influenced by pagan traditions, particularly the celebration of the spring festival in honour of the goddess Eostre. Over time, this term became associated with the Christian celebration of the resurrection, though it is not biblically or historically accurate to describe the day as such.

Thus, "Resurrection Day" or "Pascha" would more accurately reflect the true significance of the day—the victory of Jesus over death and the promise of eternal life for all who believe in Him. This shift in terminology helps to emphasize the theological meaning of the resurrection, rather than confusing it with unrelated cultural practices.

The resurrection of Jesus is foundational to the Christian faith, and yet, oftentimes, we only give it real thought around the Easter season.

But the resurrection of Jesus is so important that Paul writes, "If Christ has not been raised, your faith is futile, and you are still in your sins" (1 Corinthians 15:17). And later he says, "If in Christ we have hope in this life only, we are of all people most to be pitied" (verse 19).

In the hopes of gaining a deeper understanding of this glorious reality, here are five truths about the resurrection.

1) Jesus had a bodily resurrection.

When Jesus was raised from the dead, he didn't leave his body behind. In fact, after his resurrection his scars remained (John 20:27), he ate fish (John 20:12), he bodily ascended to heaven (Acts 1:9) and will bodily come again (1 Thessalonians 4:16). The Son of God will always have a bodily existence.

The fact that Jesus still has a body testifies to the dignity of the human body — both the ones that we have and the ones we will have after our resurrection. Matthew Lee Anderson writes, "The resurrection of the body means that to be human with God is to be with him not as disembodied souls, but as people with noses, faces, arms, and legs that are similar to those we currently have" (Earthen Vessels, 60–61).

2) Jesus had a justifying resurrection.

Perhaps the clearest instance of Paul connecting Jesus's resurrection with his justification is obscured in most English translations. Paul writes in 1 Timothy 3:16, "Great indeed, we confess, is the mystery of godliness: He was manifested in the flesh, vindicated by the Spirit, seen by angels, proclaimed among the nations, believed on in the world, taken up in glory." The word that is translated "vindicated" is typically translated "declared righteous" or "justified" elsewhere in the New Testament.

But if Jesus was perfect, how could he be justified, since justification implies guilt (see Romans 4:5)? The answer lies in Jesus's death and resurrection. Richard Gaffin explains, "As long as [Jesus] remained in a state of death, the righteous character of his work, the efficacy of his obedience unto death remained in question, in fact, was implicitly denied. Consequently, the eradication of death in his resurrection is nothing less than the removal of the verdict of condemnation and the effective affirmation of his righteousness" (Resurrection and Redemption, 121–122).

3) Jesus had a Trinitarian resurrection.

The pattern in the New Testament is to speak of God the Father as the one who does the raising, Jesus as the one who is being raised, and the Spirit as the means the Father used to raise Jesus. This pattern is seen in Romans 8:11: "If the Spirit of him who raised Jesus from the dead dwells in you, he who raised Christ Jesus will also give life to your mortal bodies through his Spirit who dwells in you."

Here, we see not only that God the Father raises Jesus through the Holy Spirit, but our resurrection will be parallel to the resurrection of Jesus — God the Father will raise us through the Spirit.

4) Jesus had a first fruits resurrection of ours to come.

Paul describes Jesus's resurrection as "the first fruits of those who have fallen asleep" (1 Corinthians 15:20). First fruits is an agricultural metaphor that points to the initial quality of the harvest. Gaffin explains, "Paul is saying here, the resurrection of Christ and of believers cannot be separated. Why? Because, to extend the metaphor as Paul surely intends, Christ's resurrection is the 'first fruits' of the resurrection 'harvest' that includes the resurrection of believers. This thought is reinforced in verse 23: 'Each in his own order: Christ the first fruits, then at his coming those who belong to Christ'" (By Faith, Not By Sight, 68).

5) In Jesus, believers are already spiritually resurrected.

The resurrection is not only a future event for believers. Those who believe in Christ have already been raised to life with him. Paul writes, "If then you have been raised with Christ, seek the things that are above, where Christ is, seated at the right hand of God" (Colossians 3:1). Christians are people who have already been raised with Christ. Gaffin explains, "[B]elievers will never be more resurrected than they already are. God has done a work in each believer, a work of nothing less than resurrection proportions, that will not be undone" (By Faith, Not by Sight, 76).

The resurrection is an already but not-yet reality for the Christian because of our union with Christ. Jesus's resurrection means that those who have faith in him have been raised from the dead because they are in Christ, and yet we still await the full experience of the resurrection to come (Romans 8:22–23).

Our faith is anchored in the resurrection of Christ, which serves as our assurance that we, too, will one day rise. The resurrection is the cornerstone of Christian hope, giving us the confidence that, just as Christ was raised from the dead, so will we be transformed. As Paul declares, "We shall all be changed, in a moment, in the twinkling of an eye" (1 Corinthians 15:52). The resurrection of Jesus affirms that death is not the end, and it gives us the hope of eternal life with Him.

In the Gospels, after Jesus rose from the dead, He appeared to His disciples and even ate fish to prove His physical resurrection. He showed them His wounds and made Himself known to them in ways that verified He was the risen Lord (Luke 24:39-43; John 20:19-29).

His resurrection was not merely a spiritual event but a bodily resurrection, which assures us that we, too, will experience a bodily resurrection in the future.

However, believing in the resurrection and experiencing the risen Christ is something deeply personal. Like Thomas, who initially doubted the resurrection, we may struggle with belief until we encounter Christ personally. When Thomas saw Jesus and touched His wounds, he declared, "My Lord and my God!" (John 20:28). It was through his personal encounter that his doubts were dispelled, and he believed.

Similarly, it is only when we personally commit our lives to Christ and devote ourselves to serving Him that we begin to truly experience the reality of His presence. The resurrection is not just an event we read about; it becomes a living reality in our own lives as we walk with Jesus daily. This personal experience with Him, in the power of His resurrection, is the most convincing evidence of His living presence with us. Just as Thomas had his moment of encounter, we, too, can experience the reality of the risen Christ in our hearts, confirming His presence and transforming power in our lives.

Christ, our risen Lord, is indeed above all, as He declared in Matthew 28:18, "All authority in heaven and on earth has been given to me." His resurrection is the foundation of our faith, as it guarantees not only our salvation but also our eternal hope. Through baptism, we are united with Christ, becoming part of His body, and we share in the one faith that Jesus is Lord and that He rose from the dead. His resurrection is the guarantee that, as He promised, He is preparing a place for us so that where He is, we may also be (John 14:2-3).

Because Jesus lives, we too can face tomorrow with hope and confidence. As the writer beautifully put it, "Because He lives, I can face tomorrow." This truth is transformative, as it grants us forgiveness of our sins and the assurance that, through Christ's life and resurrection, we too will rise to eternal life. Christ is the first fruits of the resurrection, the first to rise from the dead never to die again. He is the guarantee that all who believe in Him will experience resurrection to eternal life (1 Corinthians 15:20-22).

In John 20:14, we read about the powerful moment when Mary Magdalene, after the resurrection, encountered Jesus. She initially didn't recognize Him, but once Jesus spoke her name, she realized it was Him. "Jesus said to her, 'Mary!' She turned toward Him and cried out in Aramaic, 'Rabboni!' (which means Teacher)" (John 20:16). This intimate moment signifies that the risen Christ knows each of us personally, and when He calls us by name, we respond with joy and recognition.

The resurrection of Jesus, therefore, is not just a past event; it is a present reality that shapes our lives today. It is through His resurrection that we have the assurance of forgiveness, eternal life, and the presence of God with us. Just as Christ rose, we, too, shall rise and live with Him forever.

Verse 14: "Having said this, she turned around and saw Jesus standing, but she did not know that it was Jesus."

Yes, Mary's failure to recognize Jesus in John 20:14 highlights a significant aspect of the resurrection narrative. Her emotional distress, grief, and perhaps her blurred vision from tears could have contributed to her inability to immediately identify the risen Savior. It's a powerful image of how human emotions, like sorrow, can sometimes cloud our spiritual perception.

This scene is also a reflection of the broader truth that Jesus often appears in ways we may not immediately recognize, particularly when we are in emotional turmoil or struggling with our circumstances. His ways are higher than ours, and sometimes His presence or answer to our struggles comes in unexpected forms.

The account of the two disciples on the road to Emmaus (Luke 24:13-35) mirrors this. Though they walked and talked with Jesus for miles, they didn't recognize Him. It wasn't until Jesus "broke the bread" with them that their eyes were opened, and they recognized Him (Luke 24:30-31). This moment is rich in symbolism, suggesting that understanding and recognition of Christ often come through communion with Him—whether in the breaking of bread, prayer, or time spent in His Word.

For us today, there are moments when we may feel distant from God or fail to see His hand in our lives. Yet, just as Jesus gently revealed Himself to Mary and the disciples, He patiently and lovingly opens our eyes to recognize Him in our daily lives. When we are still, open, and willing, we can experience the presence of Jesus in ways that transcend our limited understanding, and like Mary, we can respond with joy when we finally recognize Him, saying "Rabboni" (Teacher), acknowledging Him as our risen Lord.

In the midst of our trials and deep emotions, it's important to remember that Jesus is always near, often closer than we think. Just like the disciples, we are called to recognize and remember Him, and when we do, our hearts, like theirs, will burn within us, knowing that we have encountered the living Christ.

Absolutely, that's a profound insight. In Luke 24:31, it's written that Jesus "opened their eyes, and they recognized Him." This indicates that spiritual recognition is often something that God grants in His timing, especially when our hearts are truly ready to receive the truth of who Jesus is.

For both Mary and the disciples, it was as if a veil had been lifted at the right moment. With the disciples on the road to Emmaus, it wasn't until Jesus "broke the bread" that their spiritual eyes were opened. Similarly, Mary's recognition of Jesus came when He spoke her name, a personal connection that cut through her grief and allowed her to see who was truly before her.

Your example is meaningful, too recognizing someone familiar only after they give us a clue. It's the same with Jesus. Sometimes, we're near Him without realizing it, perhaps because we're not fully open to the ways He might be speaking or revealing Himself. To truly know and recognize Jesus, we need open hearts, ready to receive Him not just as a familiar figure or prophet, but as the risen Lord and Savior.

Knowing Jesus goes beyond mere knowledge of His words or deeds; it's about embracing Him personally, understanding His role as the Redeemer, and being willing to recognize His presence in our lives. Like Mary, once we recognize His voice, our understanding of Him deepens, transforming our relationship with Him from acquaintance to a deeply personal connection with our Savior.

Verse 15: "Jesus said to her, "Woman, why are you weeping? Whom are you seeking?" Supposing him to be the gardener, she said to him, "Sir, if you have carried him away, tell me where you have laid him, and I will take him away."

Indeed, Mary Magdalene's profound grief and

shock at Jesus' death made her experience at the tomb both heartbreaking and deeply human. She was consumed with sorrow, seeking comfort in being close to His resting place, feeling the weight of loss—not only of her beloved teacher but of someone truly unique in her life. Jesus had shown her a kindness and purity she had not encountered before, a stark contrast to what she might have experienced from others. In Jesus, she found someone who saw her without judgment, who spoke truth and brought her dignity and respect.

When she found the tomb empty, it must have been another devastating blow, leaving her not only grieving but also feeling lost and uncertain about where to turn. The shock, compounded by her sorrow, seemed to cloud her senses, making it hard for her to see or hear clearly, let alone recognize the very one she sought.

But then, in a moment that changed everything, Jesus called her by name: "Mary." It was the simple act of being called personally and intimately by her name that opened her eyes to the reality that Jesus was indeed alive. This moment reveals not only the depth of Mary's love and grief but also the power of Jesus' love—a love that sees and knows each person individually.

Through this tender encounter, Mary realized that her hope, her joy, and her faith were not gone but restored. Her heart, heavy with sorrow, was lifted as she recognized her risen Lord. This moment, so personal and transformative, beautifully illustrates how Jesus meets us where we are, calling us by name, breaking through our pain and confusion to reveal His presence and His love.

Verse 16: "Jesus said to her, "Mary." She turned and said to him in Aramaic, "Rabboni!" (which means Teacher)."

The joy Mary felt in that moment must have been overwhelming—an intense mix of relief, happiness, and awe. Seeing Jesus alive after witnessing His crucifixion and thinking all was lost would have been like seeing light after the deepest darkness. Imagine expecting to find only His lifeless body, but instead, coming face to face with the risen Lord, the one who defeated death. Her sorrow instantly transformed into indescribable joy as she realized the truth: He was alive.

It's like the feeling of seeing a loved one you thought you'd lost or reuniting with someone after a long, painful separation. There's that moment of disbelief, followed by the flood of joy and gratitude that they're there with you again, alive and well. In Mary's case, though, it was even more profound, because this wasn't just a friend or family member; this was the Son of God, the one who changed her life, alive in a way that defied all human understanding.

Her encounter is a beautiful reminder of the promise of hope and life in Jesus. Just as her joy was restored upon seeing Him, the same joy is offered to all who come to know Him as the risen Savior, transforming despair into lasting hope and love.

Verse 17: "Jesus said to her, "Do not cling to me, for I have not yet ascended to the Father; but go to my brothers and say to them, 'I am ascending to my Father and your Father, to my God and your God.'

Mary Magdalene's encounter with the risen Christ in John 20:17 is a deeply moving and revealing moment that captures both the humanity of her response and the divine purpose of Jesus' mission. Seeing Jesus alive after the sorrow of His crucifixion, Mary's instinct to cling to Him reflects her love and relief—a natural human reaction to the miraculous return of someone so dearly loved.

However, Jesus' gentle instruction, "Do not cling to Me, for I have not yet ascended to the Father," highlights a significant truth about His resurrection and the unfolding of God's redemptive plan. Jesus was pointing Mary beyond the immediate joy of His resurrection to the greater reality of His ascension, where He would complete His mission by returning to the Father.

The ascension was essential for several reasons:

Presentation of the Eternal Sacrifice: As the High Priest of the New Covenant, Jesus needed to ascend to the heavenly sanctuary to present His own blood as the eternal atonement for sin (Hebrews 9:11-12). This act secured salvation for all who would believe in Him, fulfilling the sacrificial system once and for all.

Preparation for the Holy Spirit: Jesus had promised that the Holy Spirit, the Comforter, would come after His departure (John 16:7). The Spirit's coming would empower the disciples and establish the Church, marking a new phase in God's relationship with humanity.

Intercession for Believers: By ascending to the Father, Jesus took His place as our eternal mediator and intercessor, advocating on our behalf before God (Romans 8:34; Hebrews 7:25).

Establishment of His Eternal Reign: The ascension affirmed Jesus' lordship and His place at the right hand of the Father, where He reigns as King of Kings and Lord of Lords (Ephesians 1:20-22).

Jesus' response to Mary, therefore, was not a rejection but an invitation to understand the bigger picture of His mission. He was teaching her—and through her, all believers—that the resurrection was not the end but the beginning of a new reality. By ascending, Jesus would not only secure salvation but also ensure His continual presence with His followers through the Spirit.

This moment reminds us to hold loosely to

earthly expectations and to trust in the full scope of God's plan, which often surpasses our immediate understanding. Jesus' ascension assured not only His glorification but also the coming of a deeper, spiritual relationship with His followers—a relationship that transcends physical presence and invites us into eternal communion with Him.

This illustrates that even though Jesus had risen, His work was not yet complete. Only after His ascension could He fully exercise the authority given to Him, as He later declared, "All power is given unto me in heaven and in earth" (Matthew 28:18).

Jesus' instructions to Mary also remind us of that God sometimes calls us to wait, to let go, and to trust Him until His work is fully completed. Just as Jesus had to finish the work set before Him before Mary and the disciples could fully grasp His victory over death, we, too, are called to have patience and faith as God's plans unfold in His perfect timing.

Verse 18: Mary Magdalene came and told the disciples that she had seen the Lord, and that he had spoken these things unto her.

Mary's announcement to the disciples was indeed a powerful moment, filled with joy and awe. Although her message wasn't immediately received by everyone, she spoke from the undeniable experience of seeing the risen Lord. Her faith and courage in sharing this truth reflect the strength of her conviction, as she testified to the miracle of the resurrection. Through Christ's resurrection, the promise of eternal life that Jesus spoke of to Nicodemus in John 3:3 became a reality for all who would believe.

The transformation in the disciples after witnessing the risen Christ is a profound testament to the power of the resurrection. Where there was once fear and uncertainty, there was now courage, wisdom, and a deep, unwavering belief in Jesus' words. On the day of Pentecost, filled with the Holy Spirit, they boldly preached, healed, and performed miracles, showing the world that Jesus was truly alive and that He was indeed the Messiah. They spoke with an authority and conviction that came from their personal encounters with Him and the fulfilment of His promises.

The disciples' transformation and the power they demonstrated confirmed to the early church and beyond that Jesus was indeed the risen Lord. This new courage and conviction became a cornerstone of the Christian faith, as they shared the message of the risen Christ, bringing hope and the promise of salvation to all who would listen.

CHAPTER FIVE
JESUS THE SAVIOUR

The door
"Neither is there salvation in any other: for there is none other name under heaven given among men, whereby we must be saved." Acts 4:12

Just imagine this powerful and vivid analogy! The imagery of being drowning and in desperate need of rescue captures the human condition perfectly. Without Christ, we are spiritually lost, unable to save ourselves, and heading toward eternal separation from God. Salvation, as you rightly describe, is the restoration of a broken relationship with a loving and gracious God —a relationship shattered by sin but restored through the work of Jesus Christ.

Jesus' death and resurrection provide the means for this rescue. He is the lifeboat that comes to us when we are helpless. Just as the drowning person must grasp the rescuer's hand in trust, we, too, must reach out in faith, believing in Jesus as our Savior. This faith is not a work of our own but a response to God's grace—a gift freely offered to all who are willing to accept it (Ephesians 2:8-9).

Salvation is far more than a rescue from sin and death; it is also an invitation into eternal life and fellowship with God. Jesus Himself said in John 10:10, "I have come that they may have life, and have it to the full." By trusting in Him, we are not only saved from what separates us from God but also brought into the richness of a restored relationship, one that begins now and continues for eternity.

This truth beautifully highlights God's love and mercy, showing that salvation is not about our ability but about Christ's sufficiency. He is the only one who can save, the only one who can bridge the gap between humanity and God. Grasping His hand in faith leads us from the depths of sin into the eternal embrace of God's grace.

What a profound and beautiful illustration of God's redemptive work! when looking at the imagery of broken pieces and the need for the right person to restore them resonates deeply with the human experience. Like scattered fragments of something once whole, humanity is broken by sin, incapable of mending itself. This brokenness is a universal truth that touches every life, reminding us of our need for a Savior.

As you pointed out, just as a carpenter restores a table or a potter reshapes clay, Jesus Christ is the only one capable of restoring our relationship with God. He is the Master Restorer, whose work is both intricate and complete. Through His life, death, and resurrection, He gathers the broken pieces of our lives, reshaping and redeeming us into something beautiful and whole—a reflection of His grace and love.

Ephesians 2:8-9 emphasizes that this restoration is not something we can achieve on our own. It is a gift of grace, freely given and undeserved, so that no one can boast in their own efforts. This truth humbles us and glorifies God, showcasing His mercy and the depth of His love for humanity.

Isaiah 64:8 beautifully illustrates God's role as the Master Potter, shaping and moulding us according to His divine purpose:

"Yet you, Lord, are our Father. We are the clay; you are the potter; we are all the work of your hand."

This verse reminds us that through Christ, we are not simply repaired or patched up. Instead, we are completely renewed and lovingly crafted into something more glorious, aligned with God's original purpose for us. It reflects the depth of His transformative power—a restoration that makes us whole, not just functional, but thriving as His beloved children.

This renewal goes beyond fixing; it's about becoming what we were always meant to be, living fully in His grace and love.

The connection to Jeremiah 29:11, emphasizing the plans for hope and a future, reinforces the message that God's intentions for us are rooted in love and restoration.

Through His grace, brokenness is transformed into wholeness, and despair into hope. It's a powerful reminder that no matter our circumstances, His love is sufficient to renew and restore us completely. This process is indeed a testimony to His infinite mercy and faithfulness.

"And she shall bring forth a son, and thou shalt call his name JESUS: for he shall save his people from their sins." Matthew 1:21.

Jesus Christ is indeed the Savior of the world and the Author and Finisher of our faith (Hebrews 12:2). His work of salvation is unparalleled, not achieved through force or coercion, but through the power of love and the forgiveness of sins. This demonstrates the heart of God—offering redemption to all who believe, regardless of their background or past.

The truth that salvation comes through faith in Jesus is central to Christian belief. Romans 10:9-10 affirms that salvation is a matter of confessing and believing, an act of trust and surrender to the finished work of Christ on the cross and His resurrection. It emphasizes that righteousness and salvation are gifts of God's grace, received through faith, not earned by human effort (Ephesians 2:8-9).

Jesus' sacrifice cancels the debt of sin, as Colossians 2:13-14 explains: "He forgave us all our sins, having cancelled the charge of our legal indebtedness, which stood against us and condemned us; he has taken it away, nailing it to the cross." This act of grace ensures that those who place their faith in Him are not only forgiven but also reconciled to God and given the promise of eternal life.

The exclusivity of salvation through Jesus does not exclude anyone from the invitation; rather, it underscores the sufficiency of His atoning work. He is the way, the truth, and the life for all people, extending the offer of salvation to all who will believe. This message of grace, freely given and freely received, brings hope, peace, and eternal assurance to all who call on His name.

There is no one else who can save us from our sins. Jesus came that we may have life and have it more abundantly (John 10:10). He is the only way to salvation —through Him alone can we be redeemed and restored to God.

We all have a choice to make. What will you do? Will you put your faith in Jesus Christ, accepting Him as your Savior and Lord, or will you turn away? The choice is yours, but remember, salvation is found only in Him. Choose life, choose Christ, and experience the abundant life He offers.

"But this [man], because he continueth ever, hath an unchangeable priesthood." "Wherefore he is able also to save them to the uttermost that come unto God by him, seeing he ever liveth to make intercession for them." Hebrews 7:24-25

In the Old Testament, the high priest served as a mediator between God and His people, offering sacrifices for sins and entering the Holy of Holies once a year to make atonement on behalf of the nation. This priesthood, established under Aaron, was a foreshadowing of the ultimate High Priest, Jesus Christ.

Jesus, as the Eternal High Priest, surpasses the priesthood of Aaron because His priesthood is rooted in the order of Melchizedek—a priesthood marked by eternal righteousness and peace (Hebrews 7:17). Unlike the repeated and temporary sacrifices of the Old Covenant, Jesus' sacrifice was once for all, perfect and sufficient to cleanse humanity from sin (Hebrews 10:10-14). His blood, untainted by sin, fulfilled the requirements of divine justice and secured eternal redemption for those who believe.

Moreover, Jesus' role as the "door" emphasizes His exclusivity as the only path to reconciliation with God. John 14:6 underscores that salvation is not achievable through human effort, rituals, or alternate paths but only through faith in Him. This truth invites everyone to enter into a personal relationship with God through Christ, experiencing the fullness of grace, forgiveness, and eternal life.

Your reflection points to the heart of the Gospel: Jesus is both the sacrifice and the mediator, offering a way into the very presence of God. This profound truth provides hope and assurance for all who trust in Him.

"I am the door: by me if any man enter in, he shall be saved, and shall go in and out, and find pasture." John 10:9

This statement affirms that Jesus is not merely one of many ways but the only way to eternal life and reconciliation with God. His identity as the Word, present from the beginning (John 1:1), underscores His divine authority and role in the salvation of humanity.

Through His sacrifice on the cross, Jesus opened the door to redemption, offering a way for all who believe to receive the gift of eternal life. It is through faith in Him—not our works or any other means—that we are saved. His grace is the ultimate assurance for those who seek Him, providing not just a path but the only path to true and lasting life.

comforting image of Jesus as both the Door and the Shepherd! The field symbolizes the kingdom of God, a place of peace, safety, and eternal life. The fence represents God's protection, ensuring that no harm can breach His care.

Jesus standing at the doorway highlights His dual role as both the access point to salvation and the vigilant protector of those who enter. In John 10:7-9, Jesus says:

"Very truly I tell you, I am the gate for the sheep. All who have come before me are thieves and robbers, but the sheep have not listened to them. I am the gate; whoever enters through me will be saved."

This analogy reminds us of His unparalleled love and vigilance. As the Shepherd, He knows each of His sheep intimately and guards them with unwavering devotion. As the Door, He provides the only way into the field, offering not only eternal life but also the assurance that all who come to Him will be safe under His care.

Jesus is our protector, guarding us from the evil schemes of the enemy, Satan. "No man comes to the Father except by me" (John 14:6). As Ephesians 2:18-20 tells us, through Jesus, we have access to God and are made part of His eternal family. He is the only way to salvation, the only true Door, and the only protector who can safeguard us from the dangers that lie outside. Through Him, we find refuge and eternal life.

Jesus' role as our protector goes far beyond simply shielding us; it is an active and ongoing relationship of care, guidance, and empowerment. In John 10:10, He says:

"I have come that they may have life, and have it to the full."

This abundant life isn't just about safety; it's about thriving in His presence, growing in faith, and walking in the fullness of His purpose for us.

In Ephesians 6:10-18, the Apostle Paul describes the armor of God, a vivid reminder of how Jesus equips us to stand firm against spiritual attacks:

The belt of truth grounds us in Christ's unchanging Word.
The breastplate of righteousness protects our hearts through His redemptive work.
The shoes of the gospel of peace give us the confidence to share His message boldly.
The shield of faith extinguishes the fiery arrows of the enemy.
The helmet of salvation secures our identity in Him.
The sword of the Spirit, the Word of God, is our offensive weapon against lies and temptations.
Through His Spirit, Jesus actively intercedes for us (Romans 8:34) and strengthens us daily. His protection

ensures not only safety but also spiritual growth, resilience, and victory over the enemy. He doesn't just guard the door—He leads us into a flourishing life empowered by His grace.

Through faith in Christ, we are not only saved but also continually kept safe in His care. As Psalm 91:2 declares, "I will say of the Lord, 'He is my refuge and my fortress, my God, in whom I trust.'" In Him, we find true refuge—a place of eternal security where we are no longer vulnerable to the dangers of sin and separation from God.

Jesus' role as protector reassures us that we are never alone, no matter the trials we face. His love and power are more than sufficient to guard and guide us, leading us safely into the eternal presence of our Heavenly Father.

Repentance is not merely feeling regret or guilt over sin; it is a decisive turning away from sin and turning toward God. It's a change of mind, heart, and direction—a recognition that the path we're on leads to destruction and a heartfelt desire to walk in the ways of the Lord.

Just as a wise person seeks shelter when danger looms, we are called to recognize the spiritual peril of sin and run to Jesus, our refuge. He is indeed our hiding place, our fortress, and our deliverer, as Psalm 18:2 declares. He not only saves us from the eternal consequences of sin but also provides peace, protection, and strength amid life's storms.

Jesus' role as our refuge reminds us of His sufficiency. No matter how fierce the storm or how great the weight of our sin, He is able to save completely those who come to Him in faith (Hebrews 7:25). In His presence, we find forgiveness, restoration, and safety. As Isaiah 25:4 says, "You have been a refuge for the poor, a refuge for the needy in their distress, a shelter from the storm and a shade from the heat."

Repentance is the first step in finding this shelter. It is an acknowledgment of our need for God and a surrender to His will. When we repent, we turn from the path of destruction and step into the grace and mercy of Jesus, who covers us with His righteousness and protects us from the storms of judgment and separation from God.

Through repentance, we are not just saved from something—we are saved for something: a life lived in relationship with God, reflecting His glory and walking in His purpose. Jesus invites us to leave the storms behind and rest in His peace, saying, "Come to me, all you who are weary and burdened, and I will give you rest" (Matthew 11:28). When we turn to Him, we find not only refuge but also renewal, hope, and life everlasting.

What a powerful and hopeful reminder of the

saving grace of Jesus Christ! He truly is the rock of protection and the safe refuge in life's most turbulent storms. When we turn to Him, we find not only deliverance from sin and condemnation but also the assurance of His peace and presence.

Jesus' mission, as John 3:17 declares, was not to condemn the world but to save it. His coming was an act of divine love and mercy, offering forgiveness to the guilty, healing to the broken, and eternal life to the lost. He rescues us from the grip of sin and the weight of shame, lifting us out of despair and setting us on the firm foundation of His truth and grace.

The imagery of Jesus as a safe place and a refuge resonates deeply. In the storms of life—whether they are challenges, trials, or the consequences of sin—Jesus is the unshakable rock on which we can stand. As Psalm 46:1 says, "God is our refuge and strength, an ever-present help in trouble." Through Him, we find stability, hope, and the promise of a brighter future, no matter how dark the present may seem.

Jesus is also the door, the only way to salvation and reconciliation with the Father (John 10:9, John 14:6). This exclusivity of Christ as the way to God is not restrictive but rather an open invitation to all. He offers His salvation freely to everyone who believes in Him, regardless of their past or present circumstances. His love extends to all, and His arms are open wide to those who will come to Him in faith.

No matter the storm you're facing, whether it's guilt, fear, pain, or uncertainty, Jesus is the Savior who stands ready to rescue. He calls us to trust Him, to find shelter in His grace, and to experience the peace that only He can give. In Him, we are safe, forgiven, and held secure for all eternity. Turning to Jesus is not just about escaping life's storms—it's about finding life itself, abundant and eternal.

The account in Exodus 12:22 is a powerful foreshadowing of Jesus Christ, the ultimate Lamb of God. The blood of the lamb applied to the Israelites' doorposts symbolized their faith and obedience, marking their homes as under God's protection. When the death angel passed through Egypt, the blood served as a sign of deliverance, sparing their firstborn from death.

This event points directly to the sacrifice of Jesus, whose blood provides the ultimate protection and deliverance from spiritual death. As John the Baptist declared, "Behold, the Lamb of God, who takes away the sin of the world!" (John 1:29). Just as the Israelites were saved through the lamb's blood, believers are saved through the precious blood of Jesus, shed on the cross for the forgiveness of sins (1 Peter 1:18-19).

The Passover story also reminds us of the importance of faith and trust in God's provision for salvation. It wasn't the Israelites' strength or effort that saved them—it was the blood of the lamb. Similarly, we cannot save ourselves; we must trust in the sacrifice of Jesus, the Lamb of God, who delivers us from death and brings us into eternal life.

The connection between the Passover lamb and Jesus Christ highlights the continuity of God's redemptive plan throughout Scripture. It shows us that Jesus is the fulfilment of God's promise to provide a way of salvation, offering safety and deliverance to all who trust in Him.

The act of applying the blood of the lamb during the first Passover (Exodus 12:7, 13) was a powerful foreshadowing of the ultimate sacrifice of Jesus, the Lamb of God. Just as the blood of the lamb on the doorposts spared the Israelites from the angel of death, the blood of Jesus, shed on the cross, delivers us from the eternal consequences of sin and death.

In John 1:29, John the Baptist declares:
"Look, the Lamb of God, who takes away the sin of the world!"

Through His blood, we are redeemed, not just from physical death but from spiritual separation from God. As Paul explains in Romans 5:9:
"Since we have now been justified by his blood, how much more shall we be saved from God's wrath through him!"

When we accept Jesus' sacrifice in faith, His

blood is figuratively "applied" to our hearts, marking us as God's own and shielding us from the enemy's power. This covering assures us of our salvation and grants us eternal security.

The enemy, no matter how fierce, has no claim over those who are under the blood of Jesus. Revelation 12:11 affirms this victory:
"They triumphed over him by the blood of the Lamb and by the word of their testimony."

His sacrifice is the ultimate assurance of our salvation, our deliverance, and our protection, guaranteeing us a life of victory and eternal union with God.

Just as the blood of the lamb was used to protect Israel from the death angel in Exodus, so too is the blood of Jesus our protection. Jesus is the Door, and His shed blood represents the ultimate sacrifice for our sins. When we come into Christ, we are covered by His blood, just as the Israelites were covered by the lamb's blood on the doorposts. Through His blood, we are granted salvation, and we are protected from the enemy who seeks to destroy us.

Thank God that through Jesus' sacrifice, we are safe and secure, for He is the Door of our salvation. No power of darkness can harm us when we are under His protection. Through His blood, we are not only forgiven but also shielded from the attacks of the enemy. Jesus is the only way to eternal life and safety.

"Then said Jesus unto them again, Verily, verily, I say unto you, I am the door of the sheep." "All that ever come before me are thieves and robbers: but the sheep did not hear them." "I am the door: by me if any man enter in, he shall be saved, and shall go in and out, and find pasture." John 10:7-9

Jesus stands as the sole mediator between humanity and God (1 Timothy 2:5), offering the only pathway to reconciliation, salvation, and the fullness of God's promises. It is through His life, death, and resurrection that we gain access to the Father, not by our own efforts or through any other means.

By calling on Jesus, we open the Door to God's grace, mercy, and forgiveness. Without Him, there is no bridge between sinful humanity and a holy God. He doesn't just point to the way; He is the way.

This exclusivity may seem limiting, but in reality, it's a gift of clarity and assurance. We don't have to search endlessly for answers—Jesus provides the way to eternal life, the fulfilment of God's promises, and the relationship with the Father that we were created to enjoy.

Through Him, the Door remains open to all who believe, inviting them to partake in the blessings of salvation and to experience the eternal joy of being in

God's presence. Truly, there is no other way—Jesus is the only way.

The Bible is clear that Jesus is the only way to salvation. Anyone who tells you there is another way is not speaking the truth. As John 10:1-2 says, "Very truly I tell you, anyone who does not enter the sheep pen by the gate, but climbs in by some other way, is a thief and a robber." Jesus Himself said in John 14:6, "I am the way, the truth, and the life. No one comes to the Father except through me."

Any teaching or person that suggests there is another way to salvation apart from Jesus Christ is not just mistaken but misleading, as they are denying the very truth that Jesus is the only Door to eternal life. The Bible warns against such false teachings, and we are called to hold fast to the truth of God's Word, which points to Jesus as the sole means of salvation.

It is crucial to come to know Jesus as your personal Savior because it is through that relationship that you truly learn to recognize His voice. When you know Him intimately, you develop the ability to discern whether what is being said aligns with the Word of God or not. Simply learning about the Bible or being able to recite its verses is valuable, but it's the personal relationship with Jesus that transforms your understanding.

Knowing Jesus is not simply about accumulating knowledge or understanding His teachings on an intellectual level; it is about entering into a living, dynamic relationship with Him. This relationship transforms how we see ourselves, others, and the world around us. It's an intimate connection that shapes our identity and guides our decisions.

Jesus Himself emphasizes this in John 10:27: "My sheep listen to my voice; I know them, and they follow me." Knowing Him involves hearing His voice—through Scripture, prayer, and the prompting of the Holy Spirit—and responding in trust and obedience. It's about letting His truth dwell in us richly, not just as a set of doctrines but as a source of life, love, and wisdom.

This experiential knowledge of Jesus brings peace and clarity in life's uncertainties. It allows us to discern His will, stand firm in faith, and draw strength from His presence. As we walk with Him daily, we grow to understand the depth of His love—a love that casts out fear (1 John 4:18), offers rest to the weary (Matthew 11:28-30), and provides guidance in every step of life's journey (Proverbs 3:5-6).

The difference between knowing about Jesus and truly knowing Him is the difference between religion and relationship. It's not merely following rules or principles but abiding in the One who is the way, the truth, and the life (John 14:6). This relationship brings transformation because it aligns our hearts with His and empowers us to live in the fullness of His grace and purpose.

When we truly know Jesus, we experience His love in a way that moves beyond words. It becomes the foundation of our hope, the anchor of our faith, and the wellspring of our joy. This is the heart of the Christian Walk—a vibrant, growing relationship with the Savior who knows us deeply and invites us to know Him intimately.

CHAPTER SIX
JESUS THE SON OF GOD

Christ God Son

"Whosoever shall confess that Jesus is the Son of God, God dwelleth in him, and he in God." 1 John 4:15

As Christians, we are indeed called to discern truth carefully, testing any teaching against the Scriptures to determine if it aligns with God's Word. This practice ensures that our beliefs and doctrines remain grounded in biblical truth, free from deception or distortion.

Galatians 1:9 underscores the seriousness of this task, as Paul warns believers, "If anyone is preaching to you a gospel contrary to the one you received, let him be accursed." This strong admonition emphasizes the exclusivity and unchanging nature of the true gospel as revealed by Christ and taught by the apostles.

In essence, Paul's message in Galatians serves as a reminder that Jesus Christ alone is the foundation of our faith, and the message of salvation should not be altered or added to. It is essential for believers to compare all teachings with Scripture, using it as the ultimate standard. This discernment keeps our faith anchored in truth, allowing us to reject false doctrines that may lead us astray and to uphold the purity of the gospel as it was originally given.

Examining the Scriptures for ourselves is a vital practice in maintaining a faithful understanding of who Jesus Christ is, as well as in discerning truth from error. Acts 17:10-12 give a powerful example in the Bereans, who "received the word with all eagerness, examining the Scriptures daily to see if these things were so." Rather than accepting any teaching solely based on the speaker's authority, the Bereans sought to validate every message against the Scriptures, showing a dedication to truth and a reverence for God's Word.

As Christians, we are called to this same diligence. Our responsibility is to ensure that any teaching we hear aligns with the Bible's revelation of Jesus Christ. Knowing Scripture personally helps us to recognize when a message reflects God's truth or diverges from it. This requires not just passive reading but an active study—cross-referencing passages and seeking the guidance of the Holy Spirit to understand the depth of God's Word.

By becoming well-acquainted with the Bible, we are better equipped to uphold sound doctrine, avoid deception, and grow in our relationship with Christ, who is the central figure and foundation of our faith.

> If we receive the testimony of men, the testimony of God is greater; for the testimony of God is this, that He has testified concerning His Son. The one who believes in the Son of God has the testimony in himself; the one who does not believe God has made Him a liar, because he has not believed in the testimony that God has given concerning His Son. 1 John 5:9-10

Understanding who Jesus is requires us to carefully examine the Scriptures rather than simply accepting what others interpret for us. The Bible reveals the Father, the Son, and the Holy Spirit as distinct, relational persons of the Godhead, each playing a unique role in the divine purpose. Many passages affirm the reality of God as Father and Jesus as Son, and this is fundamental to Christian belief.

Jesus refers to the Father multiple times, showing the relationship between them. For example, in John 10:30, He says, "I and the Father are one," indicating unity, not an absence of distinction. Additionally, the Holy Spirit is introduced as a Counselor and Helper who will be sent after Jesus' departure (John 14:16-17), again underscoring the presence of all three persons in the Godhead.

As believers, it is our responsibility to ensure we truly understand these teachings. Scripture must be our foundation, and we are encouraged to "test the spirits" (1

John 4:1) and search the Scriptures for ourselves, as the Bereans did. This keeps our faith grounded and helps us discern truth, especially regarding foundation beliefs about the nature of God, Jesus, and the Holy Spirit. Studying and seeking guidance from the Holy Spirit to understand Scripture gives clarity on what God reveals about Himself and helps us stay rooted in true Christian doctrine.

"So, they took away the stone. Then Jesus looked up and said, 'Father, I thank you that you have heard me. I knew that you always hear me, but I said this for the benefit of the people standing here, that they may believe that you sent me.'" John 11:41-42

Jesus' prayers to the Father are indeed profound moments in Scripture, highlighting His close relationship with God and His reliance on the Father. In passages like the one where Jesus raises Lazarus (John 11:41-42), Jesus prays, saying, "Father, I thank You that You have heard Me. I knew that You always hear Me, but I said this for the benefit of the people standing here, that they may believe that You sent Me.

Whether God and Jesus are the same person cuts to the core of one of Christianity's most essential doctrines.

The Bible asserts that there is one God manifested in three distinct persons: God the Father, God the Son (Jesus Christ), and God the Holy Spirit.

They are co-equal, co-existent, and co-eternal.

While the Bible affirms Jesus is the Son of God and part of the Godhead, how does that play out in the relationship between Jesus and God the Father? This leads us to the next question, whether God and Jesus are the same person.

The short answer to this question is no.

But let me shed more light, so you can understand why this answer is no.

The difficulty arises when considering the numerous instances in the Bible and Jesus' own teachings that emphasize the distinction between God and Jesus. This distinction is not one of deity but one of role and identity. To assert that Jesus and God are the same person under modalism requires you to disregard these explicit references. We cannot reconcile modalism with the scriptural revelations that maintain the distinctiveness of Jesus and God within the context of the Godhead.

Let's consider a few scriptures highlighting the difference.

Scriptures that show God and Jesus Are Not the Same Person

In various passages throughout the Bible, Jesus continually emphasizes his relationship with the Father.

For example, he speaks of fulfilling the Father's will and following his commands. These expressions of intimacy and relationship reinforce the idea that Jesus and the Father are not the same person. Here are four scriptures to highlight.

God and Jesus present at the beginning

"In the beginning was the Word, and the Word was with God, and the Word was God. He was with God in the beginning." (John 1:1-2)

In the first verse of John's gospel, we learn something important about Jesus - that he is the Word of God. These verses tell us three essential things about who Jesus is. First, he is the Word. Second, he was with God. And third, he is God. So, in the beginning, Jesus (the Word) was there with God (the Father). John wanted to clarify that God and Jesus are not the same person, but there was a distinction between the two.

If God and Jesus were the same person, John's writing would not make much sense, and John wouldn't need to say all this. He could have just stated, "In the beginning was the Word, and the Word was God." But he deliberately emphasizes that Jesus was with God, showing they are distinct from each other, not the same person. This truth is critical in understanding the relationship between God the Father and Jesus. Furthermore, it sets the foundation for understanding the Trinity.

"Then they took away the stone from the place where the dead was laid. And Jesus lifted up his eyes, and said, Father, I thank thee that thou hast heard me." "And I knew that thou hearest me always: but because of the people which stand by I said it, that they may believe that thou hast sent me." John 11:41-42

The instances where Jesus prays to the Father, such as in John 11 when He raises Lazarus, offer deep insights into the relationship within the Godhead and the unique nature of Jesus' mission. When Jesus prays to God the Father, He isn't praying to Himself; He's expressing His unique relationship with the Father as the Son. This relationship highlights the Christian belief in the Godhead—one God in three persons: the Father, the Son, and the Holy Spirit.

The account in John 11:41-42, where Jesus raises Lazarus from the dead, is a profound moment that reveals both His divine authority and His intimate relationship with the Father:

"So they took away the stone. Then Jesus looked up and said, 'Father, I thank you that you have heard me. I knew that you always hear me, but I said this for the benefit of the people standing here, that they may believe that you sent me.'"

This prayer highlights several key truths about Jesus:

His Role as Mediator: Jesus' acknowledgment of the Father's continual attentiveness demonstrates His unique role as the Mediator between God and humanity. His prayers are always heard, affirming His sinlessness and perfect communion with the Father.

His Mission: Jesus' words emphasize that He was sent by the Father to fulfill His will, including revealing God's glory and bringing salvation to the world. By explicitly stating this, He underscores His divine purpose and origin.

Unity with the Father: This prayer reflects the unity within the Trinity—Jesus is distinct as the Son yet fully united with the Father in will and purpose. His submission is not out of inferiority but out of perfect harmony and love within the Godhead.

Building Faith in Others: Jesus prays aloud not for His own benefit but for the crowd, so they might believe in His identity and mission. His miracles were always signs pointing to His divine authority and the Father's glory.

This moment at Lazarus's tomb demonstrates Jesus' compassion, power, and purpose. It invites us to believe in Him as the One sent by the Father to bring life, not just physical resurrection but eternal life for all who trust in Him.

This pattern is also seen in other passages showing both the distinctions and the unity of the Father, Son, and Holy Spirit.

In the Garden of Gethsemane (Luke 22:42):
Jesus prays, "Father, if you are willing, take this cup from me; yet not my will, but yours be done."
This moment demonstrates Jesus' full submission to the Father's will, even in the face of unimaginable suffering. It reveals His dual nature—fully God and fully human—as He surrenders His human desires to align completely with the divine plan. It's a profound example of the harmony and trust within the Godhead.

At His Baptism (Matthew 3:16-17):
"As soon as Jesus was baptized, he went up out of the water. At that moment heaven was opened, and he saw the Spirit of God descending like a dove and alighting on him. And a voice from heaven said, 'This is my Son, whom I love; with him I am well pleased.'"
This moment showcases the Trinity in perfect unity: the Father speaks from heaven, affirming Jesus' divine Sonship; the Spirit descends, anointing Jesus for His ministry; and the Son humbly submits to baptism, identifying with humanity. Each Person is distinct in role, yet fully united in essence and purpose.

These instances emphasize that while the Father, Son, and Holy Spirit have unique roles, they work in perfect cooperation to fulfill God's redemptive plan. This unity of purpose is central to understanding the Trinity:

The Father initiates and plans (e.g., sending the Son).

The Son accomplishes and fulfills (e.g., through His life, death, and resurrection).

The Spirit empowers and applies (e.g., indwelling believers and guiding them).

Together, they reveal the beauty of God's nature and the seamless harmony within the Godhead, reminding us that our faith is grounded in this divine relationship.

In these prayers, Jesus models humility, obedience, and intimate relationship with the Father, which are foundational elements for Christian belief. Jesus' prayer life shows us the depth of His identity as the Son and affirms that, while He and the Father are one in essence, they are distinct in their persons and roles.

The instances where Jesus prays to the Father, such as before raising Lazarus, affirm the Christian belief that Jesus is not God the father but God the Son but exists as one essence in three distinct persons: Father, Son, and Holy Spirit. When Jesus looks up to heaven and addresses God as His Father, saying, "You always hear me" and "You sent me," He isn't speaking to Himself. Instead, He's demonstrating the distinct roles and relationship within the Godhead.

In John 11:41-42, Jesus says these words to show the crowd that He has been sent by the Father and that

His authority and power come directly from Him. This was essential to Jesus' mission: not only to perform miracles but to reveal His unity with the Father as the Son and to invite people to believe in Him as the One sent by God. By praying aloud, He allows those around Him to witness His connection with the Father, encouraging them to put their faith in Him as the divine Son of God.

If Jesus were merely talking to Himself, it would indeed seem confusing. Jesus is the Son who communicates with the Father, affirming both His divine mission and His obedience to the Father's will. This also reflects the self-giving love within the Father who sends the Son, the Son obeys and glorifies the Father, and the Spirit testifies to this truth in believers' hearts.

Certainly! The New Testament provides numerous passages that emphasize Jesus as the Son of God, sent with a distinct role within the Godhead. These scriptures help clarify the relationship between Jesus and the Father, underscoring His unique divine sonship, His mission, and His unity with God while maintaining distinction. Here are some key examples:

John 3:16 - "For God so loved the world that he gave his one and only Son, that whoever believes in him shall not perish but have eternal life."

This verse shows that Jesus is uniquely God's Son, sent for the purpose of salvation, a role that highlights His divine origin and special relationship with the Father.

Matthew 3:16-17 - "And Jesus, when he was baptized, went up straightway out of the water: and, lo, the heavens were opened unto him, and he saw the Spirit of God descending like a dove, and lighting upon him:" "And lo a voice from heaven, saying, This is my beloved Son, in whom I am well pleased."

Here, God the Father audibly affirms Jesus as His beloved Son, marking Him with the Holy Spirit and showing the presence of the Father, Son, and Holy Spirit at once.

Matthew 16:16-17 - "And Simon Peter answered and said, Thou art the Christ, the Son of the living God." "And Jesus answered and said unto him, Blessed art thou, Simon Bar-jona: for flesh and blood hath not revealed [it] unto thee, but my Father which is in heaven."

Jesus affirms Peter's declaration that He is the Son of God, and He attributes Peter's understanding to divine revelation from the Father, again emphasizing Jesus' unique sonship.

John 5:19-20 - "Then answered Jesus and said unto them, Verily, verily, I say unto you, The Son can do nothing of himself, but what he seeth the Father do: for what things soever he doeth, these also doeth the Son likewise." "For the Father loveth the Son, and sheweth him all things that himself doeth: and he will shew him greater works than these, that ye may marvel."

Jesus describes a relationship of perfect unity and obedience to the Father, underscoring His identity as the Son who reflects the Father's work.

John 10:30 - "I and my Father are one."

In this declaration, Jesus affirms His oneness with the Father, not only in mission but in essence. This is a profound statement of unity within the Godhead, yet with distinction in roles as Father and Son.

Hebrews 1:2-3 - "Hath in these last days spoken unto us by [his] Son, whom he hath appointed heir of all things, by whom also he made the worlds;" "Who being the brightness of [his] glory, and the express image of his person, and upholding all things by the word of his power, when he had by himself purged our sins, sat down on the right hand of the Majesty on high;"

This passage identifies Jesus as both creator and sustainer of the universe, the "exact representation" of God's being, demonstrating His divinity as well as His role as the Son.

1 John 4:14-15 - "And we have seen and do testify that the Father sent the Son [to be] the Savior of the world." "Whosoever shall confess that Jesus is the Son of God, God dwelleth in him, and he in God."

John testifies to Jesus' divine sonship and mission, underscoring that the acknowledgment of Jesus as God's Son is central to the Christian faith.

These verses collectively reinforce the concept of the three in one, showing Jesus' divinity, His distinct role as the Son, and His unity with the Father and the Spirit. They reveal a relationship based on mutual love, purpose, and unity within the Godhead.

Yes, 1 Corinthians 15:28 is a significant verse that speaks to the relationship between the Father and the Son and highlights both the Son's divine authority and His submission to the Father in fulfilling the redemptive plan. The verse states:

"When all things are subjected to him, then the Son himself will also be subjected to him who put all things in subjection under him, that God may be all in all." (1 Corinthians 15:28)

In this verse, Paul describes a moment in the future, after Christ has subdued all powers, authorities, and enemies (including death itself), when He will then turn over the kingdom to God the Father. This act of submission doesn't imply inequality or inferiority but reveals a unique aspect of the Son's role in God's redemptive plan:

Fulfilment of Mission: Jesus, as the Son, came to fulfill the Father's will, including bringing salvation, defeating sin and death, and establishing God's kingdom. His mission culminates in this act of willingly placing everything back under the Father's authority.

Distinct Roles with Unity: This verse shows the distinct roles within the Godhead. The Father initiates the redemptive plan, the Son accomplishes it, and ultimately, all things will be brought under God's reign. This does not reduce the Son's divinity but rather illustrates a difference in function within the unity.

God's All-Encompassing Glory: Paul concludes with "that God may be all in all," pointing to the ultimate purpose of creation and redemption—to bring everything into full harmony under God. This highlights God's sovereign, all-encompassing glory as the end goal of redemption.

In essence, 1 Corinthians 15:28 clarifies that Jesus, as the Son, willingly and lovingly submits His authority to the Father once His redemptive work is complete, underscoring both the unity and distinction in the Godhead. This verse reveals the profound mystery of how the Father, Son, and Holy Spirit work in perfect harmony, with each Person having unique roles in the overarching divine plan.

From Genesis to Revelation, the Bible consistently reveals Jesus as the Messiah—the Anointed One, sent by God to fulfill His redemptive plan. The promise of a Redeemer in Genesis 3:15 set the stage for God's unfolding salvation story, which finds its fulfilment in Jesus Christ. As God's only begotten Son, He came to bear the weight of our sins, reconcile us to the Father, and reveal God's love and mercy to the world.

The Bible's witness to Jesus as the Son of God is profound and undeniable. His role as the Savior, His divine nature, His teachings, His miracles, and, ultimately, His resurrection testify to His identity and purpose. Jesus is the cornerstone of our faith, the way to the Father, and the embodiment of God's grace.

The doctrine of the incarnation, as described in Philippians 2:6-8, teaches us that Jesus, while being fully God, willingly took on human nature, subjecting Himself to the limitations, sufferings, and mortality of humanity.

"He emptied Himself": This does not mean that Jesus ceased to be divine but that He voluntarily set aside the independent use of His divine privileges to fully embrace human experience. He chose to live in submission to the Father's will, modeling perfect obedience.

"For a little while" (Hebrews 2:9): This phrase highlights that the temporary nature of the Son's humiliation was part of God's redemptive plan. During His earthly ministry, the Son willingly occupied a subordinate role to the Father, not in essence but in function and position.

The Father's "Greatness" in Context

In John 14:28, Jesus says, "The Father is greater than I." This statement aligns with the understanding that the "greatness" Jesus refers to is functional and situational, not essential.

In role and circumstance: The Father remained exalted in heaven, while the Son experienced the trials of human existence. This distinction reflects their roles in redemption, not a disparity in divine essence.

In essence: Jesus is eternally equal with the Father, as affirmed in John 1:1 ("the Word was God") and Colossians 2:9 ("For in him the whole fullness of deity dwells bodily").

The Glory of Humility

Jesus' humility and obedience, even to the point of death, magnify His divine love and selflessness. By enduring suffering and taking the form of a servant, He demonstrated the extent of God's love for humanity. This humility was not a loss of divinity but an expression of it in a way that invites humanity to share in His glory.

In the resurrection and ascension, Jesus' temporary humiliation was replaced with exaltation, as Philippians 2:9 declares:

"Therefore God has highly exalted him and bestowed on him the name that is above every name."

Thus, while the Father's "greatness" was evident

during Jesus' earthly life in terms of role and position, the unity of essence between the Father and the Son remains unchanged. This truth underscores the depth of Christ's sacrifice and the glory of His redemptive work.

John writes that "the Word became flesh and dwelt among us, and we have seen his glory, glory as of the only Son from the Father, full of grace and truth" (ESV). Jesus did not cease being God; He simply took on human flesh, yet without sin (Hebrews 4:15). This is the most incredible moment in history! The omnipotent, omniscient, and omnipresent Son of God assumed a human nature and lived as one of us: He was God and man at the same time.

Jesus said, "The Father is greater than I" (John 14:28) to His troubled disciples on the night of His arrest. The uniqueness of God the Father, God the (Word) Son, God the Holy Spirit, helps explain why we are in three parts, body, Spirit, And soul. Though we are in three parts. Yet we are one person.

In the New Testament, Jesus refers to God as "Father" about 165 times. Matthew 7:21, Matthew 10:32, Matthew 10:33, Matthew 11:25, Matthew 11:26, Matthew 11:27, Matthew 12:50, Matthew 15:13, Matthew 16:17, Matthew 16:27, Matthew 18:10, Matthew 18:19, Matthew 18:35, Matthew 20:23, Matthew 25:34, Matthew 26:29, Matthew 26:39, Matthew 26:42, Matthew 26:53, Mark 8:38, Mark 14:36, Luke 2:49, Luke 10:21, Luke 10:22, Luke 22:29, Luke 22:42, Luke 23:34, Luke 23:46, Luke 24:49, John 2:16,

John 5:17, John 5:19, John 5:43, John 6:32, John 6:40, John 8:19, John 8:38, John 8:49, John 8:54, John 10:17, John 10:18, John 10:25, John 10:29, John 10:37, John 12:26, John 12:27, John 14:2, John 14:7, John 14:20, John 14:21, John 14:23, John 14:31, John 15:1, John 15:8, John 15:10, John 15:15, John 15:23, John 15:24, John 16:10, John 16:23, John 16:25, John 16:32, John 17:1, John 17:5, John 17:11, John 17:21, John 17:24, John 17:25, John 18:11, John 20:17, John 20:21, Acts 1:4, Revelation 2:27, Revelation 3:5, Revelation 3:21 Jesus said, "The Father is greater than I" (John 14:28) to His troubled disciples on the night of His arrest. Jesus had announced His imminent departure, and this puzzled them (John 13:33–38; 14:1; 16:16–18).

So according to the Bible, Jesus acknowledges God as his Father, the head, and Jesus is the Son. May this help you understand who Jesus is.

CHAPTER SEVEN
JESUS THE REDEEMER

"Forasmuch as ye know that ye were not redeemed with corruptible things, [as] silver and gold, from your vain conversation [received] by tradition from your fathers;" "But with the precious blood of Christ, as of a lamb without blemish and without spot:" 1 Peter 1:18-19

Genesis 3:15 is often called the "protoevangelium," meaning "first gospel," because it contains God's first promise of redemption. The verse states:

"And I will put enmity between you and the woman, and between your seed and her Seed; He shall bruise your head, and you shall bruise His heel." (Genesis 3:15, NKJV)

This prophecy refers to a singular "Seed" who would ultimately defeat Satan. The ultimate fulfilment of this promise came through Jesus Christ, who was born of a woman (Galatians 4:4) and would crush the power of the devil through His death and resurrection (Hebrews 2:14).

Isaiah also prophesied about the coming Messiah, the heir to David's throne: "Of the increase of His government and peace there will be no end, upon the throne of David and over His kingdom, to order it and establish it with judgment and justice from that time forward, even forever." (Isaiah 9:7, NKJV)

This was fulfilled in Luke 1:32-33, where the angel Gabriel tells Mary:

"He will be great, and will be called the Son of the Highest; and the Lord God will give Him the throne of His father David. And He will reign over the house of Jacob forever, and of His kingdom there will be no end."

This shows that Jesus is the promised Seed, the fulfilment of God's covenant with David, and the ultimate answer to the promise given in Genesis 3:15.
Yes, that's a powerful truth! The name Jesus (Greek: derived from the Hebrew Yeshua, means "Yahweh is salvation" or "The Lord saves." This name was divinely given because it directly reflects His mission —to save His people from their sins (Matthew 1:21).

Hebrews 2:14 highlights the necessity of the incarnation:
"Forasmuch then as the children are partakers of flesh and blood, he also himself likewise took part of the

same; that through death he might destroy him that had the power of death, that is, the devil."

Jesus had to fully take on humanity in order to be the perfect sacrifice. As you pointed out, only a true human being could pay the penalty for sin, but at the same time, He did not cease to be God. Philippians 2:6-8 explains this beautifully:

"Who, being in the form of God, did not consider it robbery to be equal with God, but made Himself of no reputation, taking the form of a bondservant, and coming in the likeness of men. And being found in appearance as a man, He humbled Himself and became obedient to the point of death, even the death of the cross."

This was necessary because:

Only a man could die in place of humanity. (1 Corinthians 15:21)

Only God could provide a sacrifice perfect and sufficient for all. (Hebrews 9:12)

Through His death, Jesus destroyed Satan's hold over believers. Satan's power over humanity was rooted in sin and death (Romans 6:23), but Christ's sacrifice removed that power for those who believe (Colossians 2:14-15). Now, through faith in Christ, we are no longer slaves to sin and death but have eternal life and victory in Him (Romans 8:1-2).

This truth is central to the gospel—Christ is both fully God and fully man, our Savior and Redeemer, who conquered Satan and set us free!

Yes! The many names and titles of Jesus reveal His nature, His work, and His divine authority. Each name carries deep meaning and helps us understand who He is.

One of the most powerful names given to Him is Jehovah Tsidkenu, meaning "The LORD Our Righteousness", as prophesied by Jeremiah:

"In His days Judah will be saved, and Israel will dwell safely; Now this is His name by which He will be called: THE LORD OUR RIGHTEOUSNESS." (Jeremiah 23:6, NKJV)

This name not only tells us who He is but also what He provides—God's perfect righteousness given to those who trust in Him. Since we cannot achieve righteousness on our own (Romans 3:10), Jesus becomes our righteousness through faith (2 Corinthians 5:21).

Some Other Names and Titles of Jesus:
Messiah (Christ) – "We have found the Messiah" (which is translated, the Christ)." (John 1:41)

Messiah (Hebrew) and Christ (Greek) both mean "Anointed One." He is the one chosen by God to bring salvation.
The Word – "In the beginning was the Word, and the Word was with God, and the Word was God." (John 1:1)

Jesus is the living expression of God's truth and power.

Emmanuel – "Behold, the virgin shall be with child, and bear a Son, and they shall call His name Emmanuel," which is translated, "God with us." (Matthew 1:23)

This shows His divine presence with His people.

Lamb of God – "Behold! The Lamb of God who takes away the sin of the world!" (John 1:29)

He is the perfect sacrifice for sin.

The Good Shepherd – "I am the good shepherd. The good shepherd gives His life for the sheep." (John 10:11)

He lovingly leads, protects, and saves His people.

The Alpha and Omega – "I am the Alpha and the Omega, the Beginning and the End." (Revelation 22:13)

He is eternal, the first and the last.

The King of Kings and Lord of Lords – "And He has on His robe and on His thigh a name written: KING OF KINGS AND LORD OF LORDS." (Revelation 19:16)

He reigns over all!

These names and titles reveal the greatness of Jesus and help us know Him personally. He is Savior, Righteousness, King, Sacrifice, and God with us! Our

Redeemer.

Matthew 16:23 is a powerful moment where Jesus rebukes Peter but is actually addressing Satan, who was influencing Peter's words:

"But He turned and said to Peter, 'Get behind Me, Satan! You are an offense to Me, for you are not mindful of the things of God, but the things of men.'" (Matthew 16:23, NKJV)

Satan's Influence in Opposition to God's Plan

Peter, though well-meaning, had just tried to discourage Jesus from going to the cross (Matthew 16:21-22). However, Jesus recognized that this was not just Peter speaking, but Satan working behind the scenes to try to prevent His mission of redemption. Satan had used Peter's emotions to tempt Jesus away from the suffering He must endure for the salvation of mankind.

This moment echoes an earlier encounter in Matthew 4:8-10, where Satan tempted Jesus in the wilderness, offering Him the kingdoms of the world without the cross. Jesus rejected that temptation, just as He rebuked Peter here.

God's Promise of Redemption

God's plan to restore humanity began immediately after the fall in Genesis 3:15, where He promised that the "Seed of the woman" (Jesus) would crush the head of the serpent (Satan). This prophecy set the stage for the coming of Christ, the ultimate

Redeemer.

Throughout Scripture, God continued to reveal His plan:

Isaiah 53:5 – "But He was wounded for our transgressions, He was bruised for our iniquities; The chastisement for our peace was upon Him, And by His stripes we are healed." (Foretelling Jesus' suffering for our redemption)

John 3:16 – "For God so loved the world that He gave His only begotten Son, that whoever believes in Him should not perish but have everlasting life." (The fulfilment of God's promise)

Romans 5:8 – "But God demonstrates His own love toward us, in that while we were still sinners, Christ died for us." (The proof of God's redemption in Christ)

Christ's Victory Over Satan and Sin

Through His death and resurrection, Jesus fulfilled God's promise of redemption:

Colossians 2:15 – "Having disarmed principalities and powers, He made a public spectacle of them, triumphing over them in it."

Hebrews 2:14 – "That through death He might destroy him who had the power of death, that is, the devil."

Jesus' rebuking Satan in Peter shows us that Satan's goal has always been to hinder God's redemptive plan. But God's promise of redemption was fulfilled through Christ, who willingly went to the cross, defeated sin and death, and made a way for humanity to be restored. Through faith in Him, we receive salvation and eternal life!

DR. Robert L. Reymond wrote in his book a new systematic theology of the Christian faith.

Man's greatest and most immediate need is now divine grace, which God declared he Would provide in and by a redeemer who would himself in and by his own mortal wounding finally destroy Satan's kingdom of evil by the protevangelium of Genesis 3; 15 God put into Effect the "covenant of grace" which in its Abrahamic form became salvifically definitive for all time to come

For Jesus to redeem fallen humanity, He had to become fully human while remaining fully God. This is the mystery of the Incarnation—God taking on human flesh to save us.

Jesus, Fully God and Fully Man
The Apostle John emphasizes this truth:

"And the Word became flesh and dwelt among us, and we beheld His glory, the glory as of the only begotten of the Father, full of grace and truth." (John 1:14)

Jesus did not just appear to be human—He truly became one of us. He experienced hunger (Matthew 4:2), fatigue (John 4:6), sorrow (John 11:35), and, as you mentioned, thirst:

"After this, Jesus, knowing that all things were

now accomplished, that the Scripture might be fulfilled, said, 'I thirst!'" (John 19:28)

This cry from the cross reveals His full humanity. He suffered real pain and agony, not just physically, but spiritually, as He bore the sin of the world.

Why Did He Have to Become Human?
To Represent Us – Only a human could be our substitute.

"For as by one man's disobedience many were made sinners, so also by one Man's obedience many will be made righteous." (Romans 5:19)

To Suffer in Our Place – The penalty for sin is death, and Jesus had to die for us.

"For the wages of sin is death, but the gift of God is eternal life in Christ Jesus our Lord." (Romans 6:23)

To Make Us Children of God – Through Him, we are born again into God's family.

"But as many as received Him, to them He gave the right to become children of God, to those who believe in His name." (John 1:12)

To Establish Salvation and Freedom – Through His sacrifice, we are no longer slaves to sin.

"If the Son makes you free, you shall be free indeed." (John 8:36)

Conclusion

Jesus took on human flesh so He could truly suffer, die, and rise again to redeem us. He became what we are—human—so that we might become what He is—sons and daughters of God. His incarnation, suffering, and resurrection establish our salvation, freedom, and redemption!

The work of Jesus Christ was entirely about redeeming sinners—restoring what was lost through sin and reconciling humanity to God. To fully grasp this, we must understand what redemption truly means.

What Does Redemption Mean?

Redemption, in biblical terms, means to buy back, to ransom, or to set free by paying a price. This was accomplished by Christ through His death and resurrection.

Paul explains this beautifully in Ephesians 1:7:

"In Him we have redemption through His blood, the forgiveness of sins, according to the riches of His grace."

Redemption is not just a concept—it is the full reality of what Christ achieved!

Jesus: Fully Revealed in His Redemption Work

Through His life, death, and resurrection, Jesus fully revealed:

His Divine Identity – "Declared to be the Son of God with power... by the resurrection from the dead." (Romans 1:4)

His Victory Over Sin and Death – "O Death, where is your sting? O Hades, where is your victory?" (1 Corinthians 15:55)

His Power to Save Completely – "Therefore He is also able to save to the uttermost those who come to God through Him." (Hebrews 7:25)

The Final Blow to Sin's Power

Jesus delivered the final and ultimate blow to sin, death, and Satan. His resurrection proved that He absolutely, completely, and fully demonstrated the divine life. He didn't just offer temporary relief—He fully secured eternal redemption:

Colossians 2:14-15 – "Having wiped out the handwriting of requirements that was against us... He has taken it out of the way, having nailed it to the cross. Having disarmed principalities and powers, He made a public spectacle of them, triumphing over them in it."

Hebrews 9:12 – "Not with the blood of goats and calves, but with His own blood He entered the Most Holy Place once for all, having obtained eternal redemption."

Conclusion

Redemption is not just an idea—it is a finished work in Jesus Christ. He paid the price, defeated sin, and opened the way to eternal life. He is now fully revealed as the Son of God, the victorious Redeemer, and the King of Glory!

CHAPTER EIGHT
RELATIONSHIP WITH JESUS

"And I will pray the Father, and he shall give you another Comforter, that he may abide with you for ever;" "Even the Spirit of truth; whom the world cannot receive, because it seeth him not, neither knoweth him: but ye know him; for he dwelleth with you, and shall be in you." John 14:16-17

"Spirit of Christ" is indeed another name for the Holy Spirit, emphasizing the close relationship between Jesus and the Spirit (Romans 8:9–11). It reflects the idea that the Spirit continues the work and presence of Christ in the believer and in the world.

Parakletos, used in the Gospel of John (especially John 14–16), is rich in meaning. Besides "helper," it can also be translated as advocate, comforter, or counsellor. The term suggests someone who comes alongside in support—legally, emotionally, or spiritually.

The Spirit is not merely a force or an influence, but a person, co-equal and co-eternal with the Father and the Son. The Spirit glorifies Christ, teaches believers, convicts the world, and empowers the Church.

As you are redeemed, you begin to build a relationship with Christ.

Through that redemption, you are transformed—your old self passes away, and the Holy Spirit comes to dwell within you. From that moment on, you're no longer walking alone; you now have a personal, living relationship with Jesus Christ.

This transformation is not just spiritual—it affects your entire being.

Your thinking begins to shift. Your heart becomes more sensitive to God's presence. Your understanding deepens, opening your eyes to what God expects of you.

You begin to desire what He desires. You start to see the world differently, through the lens of grace and truth. And as you walk with Him daily, your life becomes a testimony of His love, mercy, and power.

"Whosoever shall confess that Jesus is the Son of God, God dwelleth in him, and he in God." —1 John 4:15

This confession is not just words—it's a declaration of faith, of surrender, and of new life.

When someone truly confesses Jesus as the Son

of God, it marks the beginning of a divine relationship. God takes residence in them, and they are united with Him. It's not about religion—

It's about a relationship.

Through this relationship, the Holy Spirit moves in, bringing transformation from the inside out. Thoughts begin to align with God's truth.

Desires start to reflect His will. And understanding opens like a door, revealing who God is and what He calls us to be.

This is the mystery and the beauty of redemption: God doesn't just save you—He dwells with you. He makes you, His home.

Many people question the existence of the Father, the Son, and the Holy Spirit.

They may try to reason it away, debate it, or deny it altogether.

But to truly know who Jesus is, it takes more than head knowledge—it takes relationship.

You must come into relationship with Him. And it is the Holy Spirit who reveals Christ to your heart, just as He did with Peter. Jesus said to Peter, "Flesh and blood has not revealed this to you, but My Father who is in heaven." (Matthew 16:17)

That kind of revelation doesn't come from argument or intellect—it comes through spiritual intimacy. When you walk with Jesus, when you seek Him, the Holy Spirit will make Him known to you.

And when you know, truly know, who He is— no one can tell you otherwise. No doubt can shake you. No lie can deceive you. Because you'll understand, deep in your spirit, who the Bible says Jesus is: The Christ, the Son of the Living God. Savior. Lord. King. The Word made flesh.

The indwelling of the Holy Spirit is what truly sets the believer apart, not just in terms of outward behaviour or intellectual agreement, but in the inner transformation that takes place when a person is united with Christ.

As Paul writes in Romans 8:9:
"You, however, are not in the flesh but are in the Spirit, if indeed the Spirit of God lives in you. And if anyone does not have the Spirit of Christ, they do not belong to Christ."

This verse makes it clear—what distinguishes the believer is not merely belief or action, but the presence of the Spirit of God within.

The Spirit's Role in the Believer:
Strengthens our faith: The Spirit helps us in our weakness, interceding for us (Romans 8:26), and continually reminds us of who we are in Christ.

Assures us of our adoption: Through the Spirit,

we cry "Abba, Father," and know that we are children of God (Romans 8:15-16).

Guides and sanctifies us: The Spirit leads us into all truth (John 16:13) and works within us to make us more like Christ.

Marks us as God's own: The Holy Spirit is the guarantee, or seal, of our inheritance (Ephesians 1:13-14).

This inner presence is the evidence of new life. It's not about striving in our own strength but living in relationship with God through the power of His Spirit. The Holy Spirit enables us to live differently, not as a performance, but as a fruit of our union with Christ.

So yes—what truly distinguishes the believer is the presence and power of the Holy Spirit. It is He who transforms hearts, convicts of truth, and empowers us to live lives that reflect the glory of God.

Marriage, at its heart, reflects the deep, selfless love that Christ has for His Church—a love that puts the other person first. As Paul writes in Ephesians 5:21, "Submit to one another out of reverence for Christ." That mutual submission is the foundation of a healthy, Christ-centered relationship.

Whether you're a husband or wife, your role is

not about dominance or control—it's about love in action:

You protect, not just physically, but emotionally and spiritually.

You stand by each other in every season—through joy and sorrow, success and struggle.

You choose daily to serve, to encourage, and to build each other up.

You find joy in your partner's joy, and peace in their peace.

You give, not just when it's easy, but especially when it's hard—because love is a covenant, not a contract.

This kind of love mirrors Christ's sacrificial love for us. In marriage, it's not about keeping score, but about out-giving one another in grace and kindness. That's the beauty of two people becoming one—carrying each other's burdens, sharing each other's dreams, and walking through life hand in hand, with God at the center.

That kind of passionate, all-in love is such a powerful reflection of the depth of devotion we're capable of when our hearts are truly committed. When someone says "yes" to you—chooses you—you don't take that lightly. Something awakens inside you, and you rise to the calling of love with boldness, like a soldier ready to protect, provide, and give you all.

You'd go to the ends of the earth if it meant bringing them joy, comfort, or peace. You'd work tirelessly not because you must, but because you want to. Because love fuels effort. It drives sacrifice. It brings out the best in you.

And then, think about this—that's how God loves us, but even deeper.

We say "yes" to Him by faith, but He chose us first. And when He did, He didn't hold anything back. He gave everything, even His life.

Romans 5:8 put it this way:
"But God demonstrates His own love for us in this: While we were still sinners, Christ died for us."

If we are willing to go all out for someone we love on earth, how much more should we cherish and respond to the One who went all out for us from heaven?

That love—whether in human relationships or in our relationship with God—isn't passive. It acts. It protects. It pursues. And it always seeks the good of the other.

When we grasp the magnitude of God's

sacrifice, it should stir something deep within us. It's not about earning His love—it's about responding to it. When we truly give our lives to Him, we're not just adding Him into our routines—we're entering into a covenant relationship where devotion, obedience, and love become our joyful response.

He gave everything for us. So, when we give our lives to Him, our priorities shift. Our desires change. We begin to live with purpose, and that purpose is centred around pleasing the One who loved us first.

Micah 6:8 says it so clearly:
"He has shown you, O man, what is good. And what does the Lord require of you?
To act justly, and to love mercy, and to walk humbly with your God."

This isn't complicated theology—it's relational truth. God tells us exactly what He desires:

Act justly – Do what is right, even when it's hard.

Love mercy – Be generous in forgiveness and compassion.

Walk humbly with your God – Stay close to Him, depend on Him, and never forget that it's all by His grace.

Living to please God doesn't mean perfection—it means direction. It means daily turning your heart toward Him, asking, "Lord, are You pleased with my life today?"

Because when you love someone, you want to please them.
And when you love God, the One who gave everything for you, nothing less than full devotion feels right.

that's the heart of true relationship with Jesus. It's not just belief, it's devotion. It's not just a moment of salvation, but a life surrendered. When you understand who He is and what He's done—how He laid down His life for you—the only fitting response is to give Him your day, your night, your everything.

It doesn't matter what others think, or what the world says.
What matters is:

Are you living for the One who died for you?

Are you walking in a way that reflects the love you claim to have for Him?

And then comes the honest self-examination:

"Can I truly say I have that relationship with

Christ?"

"Am I living each day to the best of my ability to follow in His footsteps?"

Not perfectly—but wholeheartedly.
Not out of duty—but out of love.
Not because you're trying to earn grace—but because grace has already found you, and now your life is a thank-you letter to God.

Jesus said in Luke 9:23:
"Whoever wants to be my disciple must deny themselves and take up their cross daily and follow me."

It's daily. It's intentional.
It's not about rules—it's about relationship.
And that relationship calls for everything, because He gave everything.

If you're ever unsure, the beautiful thing is—you can always come back. Jesus is never far. He welcomes the heart that says, "Lord, I want to live for You again. Fully."

You can't truly know who Jesus the Christ is apart from the Word of God. The Scriptures are the divine revelation of who He is—from Genesis to Revelation. They speak of Him, point to Him, and glorify Him. Jesus Himself said in John 5:39:

"You search the Scriptures because you think that in them you have eternal life; and it is they that bear witness about me."

If we claim to follow Christ, then we must also be students of His Word. Because unless we study, we won't know—not truly. And without knowing Him through the Word, how can we follow Him in truth?

Do you know Him as the Son of God? Do you know Him as Savior, Redeemer, King, and Friend? Have you hidden His Word in your heart, like Psalm 119:11 says? "I have hidden Your word in my heart, that I might not sin against You."

The Holy Spirit is our teacher. He takes the written Word and breathes life into it, illuminating our hearts so we don't just read about Jesus—we encounter Him.

Without the Scriptures, your knowledge of Christ is incomplete. Without the Spirit, your understanding remains veiled. But together, the Word and the Spirit open our eyes, deepen our faith, and anchor our relationship with Jesus in truth.

So, the question stands:

Do you really know Jesus—or just know about Him? Have you sat with His words? Let them shape you, convict you, lead you? Because to know Him truly is to love Him fully. And to love Him is to desire His Word like daily bread.

Many people strive to live morally, to be kind, fair, and even reverent. Some may even love the teachings of Scripture and try to follow biblical principles. But as you so rightly pointed out—morality is not salvation, and religion is not the same as relationship.

Living a good life is admirable, but it is not what saves us. Salvation is not about how good we are; it's about who Jesus is and whether we have received His life within us.

Jesus said in John 3:6: "That which is born of the flesh is flesh, and that which is born of the Spirit is spirit."

No amount of good works, religious habits, or scriptural knowledge can give us spiritual life. That life only comes from God's Spirit living within us—when we're born again through faith in Christ.

As Paul writes in Romans 8:9: "If anyone does not have the Spirit of Christ, they do not belong to Christ."

It's sobering, but it's also freeing—because it means that salvation is not something we can earn. It's a gift, received by grace through faith, and confirmed by the indwelling presence of the Holy Spirit.

So yes, someone can be: Concerned about

justice yet not be saved.

Devoted to scripture, yet not alive spiritually. Religious in routine, yet still empty inside. But when the Spirit of God comes into a person, everything changes.

They don't just know about God—they know Him. They don't just try to live right—they are empowered to. They don't just read the Word—they hear God through it.

The question we all must ask is not, "Am I good?" or "Am I religious?"

But rather, "Have I been born of the Spirit?" "Is Christ truly living in me?"

this is the core of the Christian life. Galatians 2:20 is one of the most powerful declarations of identity and surrender in all of Scripture:

"I have been crucified with Christ, and I no longer live, but Christ lives in me. The life I now live in the body, I live by faith in the Son of God, who loved me and gave Himself for me."

To be crucified with Christ means more than just believing in Him—it means dying with Him. It means that your old self, your sin nature, your desire to live independently from God—has been nailed to the cross. That's not symbolic language—it's spiritual reality for the believer.

It means: You are no longer under the law, trying to earn God's favour through works. The power of sin has been broken—not that you never sin again, but sin no longer has dominion over you. Your life is no longer about you—it's about Christ living in you.

The question is a piercing one:

Can you say with confidence: "I am crucified with Christ"?

That means you're not clinging to your old ways or living a double life. It means: You've surrendered your identity to Him. You walk by faith, not by sight. You trust not in your strength, but in His life now working through you.

It's a place of deep surrender, but also deep power—because when you die to self, Christ lives through you. And that's freedom.

If you're living this way, it's not about perfection, it's about direction. It's the ongoing daily choice to say: "Not my will, but Yours." "Not my life, but Yours in me."

what a beautiful and powerful call to deep, living relationship with Jesus the Christ. This is more than religion. It's more than ritual. It's about a living, breathing relationship with the risen Savior, the centre of our lives, the light that shines through us, the truth that transforms us.

When we truly walk with Jesus: We are glorified in Him—not with worldly fame, but with the radiant glow of His presence in our lives.

We become lights—not just for our own path, but as beacons to others, pointing them toward the narrow way that leads to life (Matthew 7:14).

We become vessels of immortal life, not because we are worthy, but because His eternal life now lives in us. "Trust Jesus the Christ who is the living centre of the Christian life."

Yes—He is not on the sidelines. He is not an add-on. He is the heart, the pulse, the very life of who we are.
And it's through Him—by faith, by the Spirit—that we draw the blessings of the Gospel deep into our own souls and make the truth our truth, God's truth living in us.

About the Author

Reverend Peter Husbands, started from very humble beginnings. He was born on the beautiful island of Barbados, and grew up in the second largest town on the island, Speightstown. From the tender age of 11, Peter's foundation was built in the church in the Grange Pentecostal House of Prayer and Passage Road St. Micheal.

In 1985, Peter moved to England and joined the Church of God in Christ. After a few years, Peter began studying at the Urban Divinity Bible College, where he earned a diploma and a certificate in advanced Pastoral Studies. His dedication to education and leadership led to him being awarded the title of "elder" by the college.

After many requests to preach at various churches, both in Barbados and England, Peter was invited to become the pastor of Shiloh Church of the Lord Jesus in 2019. Peter humbly accepted this call as service to our Lord Jesus Christ and has served in this capacity ever since.

www.ingramcontent.com/pod-product-compliance
Lightning Source LLC
Chambersburg PA
CBHW060357080526
44583CB00012B/353